Love Letters from Your Life is part invita
and show up, to reflect and release, to be
And it's part invocation—an intentional a
to live deliberately, fearlessly, and above all lovingly, toward
ourselves and others. *Love Letters* creates a practical and
powerful framework to help you think, act, live, and lead with
light, all in support of our collective mission to "love onward!"

– Deanna Davis, PhD Author of *The Law of Attraction
in Action* and *Living With Intention*

Life can get frustrating, scary, and dark. Through stories, letters
from life and some very insightful action steps, Marci Moore
and Mary Anne Radmacher guide you to a positive, uplifting
new approach to living. Marci became one of my heroes when
she stared down cancer with unwavering optimism, hope and
strength. Now she shares a coping strategy that will give those
superpowers to you. This book will change your life if you let it.

– Fawn Germer, Best-selling, Oprah-featured
author and global keynote speaker

In *Love Letters From Your Life*, Marci and Mary Anne's
encouraging letters and original stories illuminate the
enormous power LOVE has to change our lives and
ultimately the world. Each love letter and story felt like
my heart and soul were taking a beautiful walk together
holding hands. I came away inspired with new ideas to
create a deeper wave of love in my own life and the world.

– Caren Albers, author of *Happiness Junkie*

This book is an uplifting reminder of how important it is to
see ourselves and others—*really* see. Us. All of us. In a world
where too many of us are looking down at our cell phones
instead of what is going on *in* and around us, Marci Moore and
Mary Anne Radmacher, through their parabolic stories and
personal 'Letters from Life' to the reader, brilliantly nudge us to
look up, listen, and love ourselves and all who cross our path.

– Lisa Vetter, Author and CEO of Tour de force Speakers

These letters are filled with accessible, practical wisdom—a delightful combination of gentle reminders and bold proclamations. Find a YES for these letters so they can help you expand your possibilities.

– Paul Wesselmann, writer, educator, seeker

Love Letters From Your Life by Marci Moore and Mary Anne Radmacher, is a delectable pairing of life lessons and love. As if attending a fine wine tasting and pairings dinner, you will mull over the flavors as you realize the beauty in the duo of author's wisdom and life experiences. The richness of life's love letters encourages you to press onward and learn more, while the honesty and heart in the stories enhances each bite of kindness and sip of hope. A perfect pairing you deserve to gift yourself; with an impact that will linger in that way that brings out the best of you.

– Jeanette Richardson Herring, Artist/Author and Arts Advocate

Love Letters from Your Life is a source of simple wisdom from the heart, supported by practical ways to practice and live that wisdom. It is a book you could skim and still gain much from, or dive deep into and explore the pathways of your heart to create change in your life and the world around you. As gratitude is a theme woven among the pages, let me offer my gratitude for this gift of love.

– Lynda Allen, Poet, Author, Life in progress

Love Letters from Your Life is a wonderfully warm and open-hearted book that uses extensive personal memoir as a teaching tool for living a life of love, personal adventure, acceptance, forgiveness, and celebration, even in the face of heartbreak. There are also many exercises that offer the reader an intricate network of questions to inspire the exploration of values, commitment and choices in areas such as self-nurture, self-discovery, focusing your attention, being a good neighbor, and the power of forgiveness and gratitude. Used fully, these exercises could guide a lifetime of personal growth. This book offers a path to rediscover love, rediscover kindness, and rediscover yourself. Marci and Mary Anne are true champions of the soul.

– Jonathan Lockwood Huie, author of self-awareness books

Mary Anne (Em) Radmacher's poetic voice rings through these letters from your life, beautifully augmented by Marci Moore's deep knowing about the clarion call of the heart we all experience— if we can allow ourselves to feel it. This book is truly a gift from the inner voice of the heart, taking us on a journey and providing not only landmarks, but potent questions to guide our way.

– Patti Digh, Author of *Life is a Verb* and *The Geography of Loss,* among other books and founder of Life Is A Verb camp.

In a fast-paced world, *Love Letters from Your Life* shows up with centered instruction that provides clear focus on what matters. Marci Moore is one of the most truly grounded and loving souls you will ever meet—and her impact is HUGE. But she's no mountain top guru. She teaches us how to love in the middle of corporate life, stress with your spouse, and how to become a global citizen of love, in simple, yet palpable ways. Combined with Mary Anne Radmacher's singular creative brilliance, this book will give you hope for humanity—and make you want to be the best version of yourself possible.

– Tama Kieves, USA Today featured visionary career coach, and bestselling author of *Inspired & Unstoppable* and *Thriving Through Uncertainty.*

Life is a love letter from the Divine—a letter overflowing with beauty, joy, wonder, and discovery. And the parts that don't feel like love? They are sacred invitations to *be* love. Marci Moore's heart-filled narrative calls us to remember that we are here to be a love letter to the world. Our "job" is to show up in love and as love, discovering in each moment fresh new ways to be love.

– Janet Conner, prayer artist, host of Praying at the Speed of Love podcast, and author of *Writing Down Your Soul* among others.

Love Letters From Your Life

Inspired Ways to
Show Up with Love

By

MARCI MOORE

With Love Letters and
Contributions by

MARY ANNE RADMACHER

Published by:
Innergized!, Inc.
PO Box 7147
Seminole, Florida 33775

Printed in the United States of America

Interior Layout Design by
Euan Monaghan of Standout Books

Photography by Cast and Forge Photography

Cover Design by Nicole Pransky

ISBN: 978-1-7331471-0-1

Dedication

From Marci Moore:

You will observe that my wife, Pam Williams, unfolds many of my life stories, right alongside me. When I use the term "we," unless I am specifically talking about another individual, you can be sure the "we" refers to Pam and me. So this is the place to tell you a little about Pam. She is my wife and the love of my life. We've worked together for 25 of the past 29 years in the nonprofit arena, 21 years in our own consulting practice centered on turning around non-profits in financial crisis.

We've been a couple for 24 magical years. Pam is energetic, kind, thoughtful, generous and intelligent with a wicked sense of humor. She is a great stoker on the back of our tandem bicycle. She's also the social director, smiling and waving at everyone she sees. Pam is an extrovert and I'm an introvert. We are blessed to have a love that grows deeper and sweeter with time. Sometimes I almost pinch myself to make sure it's real. We are the kind of couple people tell, "I want some of what you have" because after all this time, the love we have for one another is that obvious. I believe it's because of the strong foundation of love in our home that we are both able to love even larger in the world today.

From Mary Anne Radmacher:

Laurie Foley and Ralph Bramucci showed up to all their days with love. I wrote these letters for them, for the people they loved on and for you.

Table of Contents

Preface

When I began writing Love Letters From Your Life over five years ago, I imagined it would target a certain segment of the population, those wanting to do and be more when it came to showing up with love for themselves and others. I wanted to get this message out into the world quickly, but God had other plans. In late 2016, I was diagnosed with breast cancer. That journey lasted far longer than I expected.

My journey with cancer is a long road. The extensive chemo treatment I received destroyed the new neural pathways I had to recreate over a lifetime after a traumatic brain injury in my teens. I spent another year beyond post chemo and radiation in brain rehab, both at the Brain Fitness Center and in my own home. During the delay, the world changed.

Let's face it. Life is more challenging than it was a few years ago. We live in a frenetic world. We're more connected than ever before yet somehow, more disconnected. We're likely to let phone calls go to voice mail and avoid returning or making them at any cost. We spend more time online than with the people sitting right next to us, in the next room or living next door. Even on public transportation, we're transfixed by our devices. I'm not against technology; I am a huge proponent of love. And when it comes to love, presence matters.

When I ask myself What's missing? the answer always comes back, love and more love—self-love and love of others—those we know and those we've yet to meet. Love is what strengthens us and our society, yet when we watch the news these days, it seems to be missing in action.

I believe God purposefully held up the publication of Love Letters From Your Life because H/She knew the timing wasn't right. Today, we need your love in the world more than ever. We need to wish for others what we wish for ourselves—to feel accepted, safe and loved, wherever we go. To be cared about, acknowledged, embraced, encouraged and uplifted. To be fully seen as human beings, children of God/Spirit no matter our gender, ethnic heritage, race, citizenship status, sexual orientation or religion.

I never imagined that asking people to show up with love would be necessary, but it is.

We are inviting you to join us now on the path to loving larger than you've ever loved before. Please say yes, with all of your heart.

Love Onward,

Marci Moore

Introduction

Marci Moore

I tell most of the stories in this book. They are each rooted in my life experiences and reflect my lifelong commitment to show up with love. I don't qualify showing up with words like "perfectly" or "well timed." Sometimes, just showing up with loving intent is a true victory. Perfectly. Imperfectly. Love is love. Bringing your most loving self to the world that you inhabit is what matters. These stories, many of them based in some of the most difficult circumstances of my life, are written to inspire you. To find the love in the midst of joy and in the midst of hardship. I hope this book inspires you to find and tell your own amazing stories regarding how you bring love to all of your days.

We are all just one story away from the changes we long to make in our lives.

Stories help us make sense of that which seems nonsensical. From the life experiences we share with each other, we learn, we inform our own events and we fashion new and more rewarding ways of navigating the world. This book is a collection of stories and love letters that will connect you to a more loving life experience.

> "That's just life sending you a little love letter."
> *Mary Anne Radmacher*

I remember an adult saying that to me when I was a child. It made quite an impression on me. When circumstances beyond my control (and really, what circumstances aren't?) would come to my days, I would reflect on that little bit of wisdom.

What if it were so? What if all the circumstances we come across and the events we experience really are a form of loving communication from our life? It allows even the most difficult of events to be considered in a bigger context. *Love Letters From Your Life* contains important stories that we share when we are looking to illustrate a key lesson in life or to demonstrate that the seemingly inexplicable can turn out to be a thread in a larger, and often, beautiful tapestry.

Chapter One: Reflect

Give yourself a pep talk, shout an unreserved YES!
into this vast universe, pull the ripcord and launch
into the day ready for this adventure called love.

—*Marci Moore*

Dear You,

I feel you. I understand your pace, the press and the
overwhelming compulsion to do all of the things on
your list. You work so hard. Every day. It might feel
impossible when I keep suggesting that you take time
to reflect. Let me be a little more practical and maybe
that will help. First? Just pause. Pausing to reflect
is just like reading the Cliff Notes on the story of
your day. Taking those moments to consider the flow,
the places where there was no flow and the events of
your experience is a grand efficiency. Reflection in
this moment tutors you for tomorrow. It allows you to
identify the things you want to eliminate and those
which bear repeating. Most importantly, reflection
invites more of the goodness into your life. It's a
moment that opens the gates to gratitude. One of the
best outcomes from moments of reflection is a deeper
appreciation of your own skills, talents and efforts.
I'll keep reminding you of the worth of setting aside
just this bit of study time.

Love,

Your Life

Reflection has been a necessary part of my life for as long as I can remember. With four brothers, two parents and numerous pets living alongside me in the one room lakefront cottage we shared for four years, space for reflection was virtually nonexistent. I often stayed awake long after the house quieted each night so I could hear myself think. It was during those nighttime reflections that I dreamed of quiet spaces, a room of my own and writing.

Later on, that ability to reflect gave my eleventh-grade self the courage to approach my parents with a hard truth. "I'm failing most of my classes. I really messed up this semester. I want to transfer to night school. I will graduate. I promise." They had no reason to believe me but together they marched me down to school and withdrew me. I graduated a full semester ahead of my class. Reflection allowed me to learn from my adolescent missteps and ushered me into adulthood relatively unscathed. I still need reflection today.

The practice of self-reflection is a daily invitation to know yourself intimately. Reflection is just that—it's not blaming nor personal recriminations, but examining yourself with abundant curiosity. It's looking deeply within, acknowledging where you stand, examining what's gotten you to this point and sometimes asking, "What's next?" It's a genuine willingness to peel back the layers of your inner self, separate facts from feelings and ask yourself what you most need right now or who you need to be in a given situation. It's looking at yourself stripped bare, not only seeing your reflection in that deep shimmering pool but diving in to retrieve what lies hidden beneath the surface—the whole of who you are. Reflection takes courage.

Reflection is an ingrained practice for me, much of which takes place in the form of journaling each morning. There I examine the previous day, noting gratitudes, celebrations, learnings, life experiences and events in the larger world, often contemplating my response and responsibility to them. I review my relationships, asking if I've been the wife, daughter, sister, aunt and friend I've committed to be. Through reflection, I regularly discover instances where I could have been better.

The practice of reflection saves us from ourselves. My poorest decisions were birthed during the absence of reflection, my best, the result of fearless dives beneath the surface.

Whether your preferred practice is prayer, meditation, long walks, listening to quiet music or journaling, you need purposeful time for reflection to ponder the bigger meaning of your life. While that might sound pompous or grandiose, the meaning of your life is a weighty topic. Far too many of us get to the end of our lives with garbage bags stuffed full of regrets. This isn't about wishing you'd climbed Mount Everest or skydived or spent your time in a monastery; this is about what you did with your allotment of hours here on earth. This is about how you mattered to others.

Reflection begets discoveries. Discoveries invite action and sometimes, necessary change.

This is your starting place, your chance to set your intention for the rest of our time together.

Try This:

1. How do you currently make room in your life for personal reflection? Journal about your experience with reflection. When I say "journal," please know that if you are more comfortable making a list of explorations or a list of questions, do that.
2. What has been the most obvious benefit of deep reflection in your life? Journal about the benefits of reflection in your life.
3. Begin a week-long intentional reflection practice. Starting today, choose how and when you will engage in daily reflection. If the time or location doesn't work for you, select an alternative for week two. Keep adapting your practice until you land on one that resonates with you.
4. At the end of your daily reflection, take a few minutes to capture any lessons that surfaced for you. Sometimes reflection results in a deep knowing or certainty about an issue in your life. When necessary, make time to explore these thoughts further.

Listen to Yourself

Listen to your heart, it will guide you on the right path.

—*Lailah Gifty Akita*

Dear You,

There's a lot of noise around here, isn't there? Technology. Voices rising above each other in order to be heard. The whisper of memories, the whine of regret and the whir that sounds like anxiety asking, "What if?" All that noise makes listening to yourself like hearing an ice cube hit the cement at the bottom of the 9th, all runners on bases at a baseball game. I'd be fooling you if I told you there was a physical oasis of quiet in the midst of modern life. Even when the lights are out, the electrical current in a home still hums.

What I offer you, instead, is the sanctuary you carry around within you. Inside is your very own still, small voice. It is your deepest truth, your highest knowing and it is ready to speak to you and, in fact, speaks to you all of the time. You often call it your first impulse. And when you don't act on it you are likely to say, "I KNEW it... that was the first thing I thought."

Remember your first things. They are your core compass and the manner in which they rise up in thought, through impulse or word, is your very own True North. That small voice is always speaking to you: Train yourself to listen.

Love,

Your Life

Listening to your inner voice requires a deliberateness of purpose, now more than ever. Distractions abound, increasing daily. We're connected to the world 24/7/365 and the sheer volume of messages and interruptions relentlessly competes with family, friends, co-workers and day-to-day responsibilities for your attention. Without consciously creating space, it's likely you'll miss some important messages.

For several years I functioned on autopilot, tolerating a life I'd abdicated to my former partner. I'd silenced my inner voice to keep from losing my mind. Spirit knew I'd put my heart on hold but patiently waited for space to be heard. The door cracked open on a road trip to Texas when an innovative business opportunity caught my attention, reintroduced possibility and renewed my enthusiasm for life. That excitement yanked me firmly into the present, inviting me on a life-changing listening journey. Something within me shifted. On the long drive home, I tuned into Spirit and began listening with interest.

For the next year, I spent an hour each evening lounging in a hot bath, escaping the perpetual background of canned sitcom laughter and opening myself to Spirit's voice. Sometimes I asked questions out loud and invited the answers in. Other times I asked for signs, confirmation that I was on the right track—especially when I first began listening again. Slowly I found my way back to myself.

Sometimes Spirit whispers so softly we may question whether we heard anything at all. Eventually, the whispers grow stronger.

Our role is simple. Listen. Make space for what we most need to hear. Our inner voice speaks when there is something to be said, nudges us with truths, awakens us to greater awareness, connects us to others, plugs us in where we most belong and provides guidance when we've lost our way.

Spirit comes to us in many different forms. Before Pam and I became a couple, a vivid dream forced me to acknowledge what I'd been reluctant to admit—even to myself. In it, I stood in front of Pam, crying and asking, "What if you finally meet the right person but it is 10 years too late?" With those words, I woke up sobbing. Because Spirit gave me the courage to speak up, this year we celebrate our twenty-fourth anniversary. Thank God for persistently knocking until I finally listened.

Listening means paying attention to our bodies, too. After putting in many consecutive years of nonstop, around-the-clock business turnaround work, Pam's body stopped saying yes. Exhaustion and pain became constant companions. She spent weeks barely able to move from bed to sofa and back again. After she began listening to her doctor and her brilliant inner voice, it took another two years of rest, exercise and restoration before she finally started feeling like herself.

> *Spirit guides us in positive, uplifting directions and continually has our highest good at heart. Give Spirit the best chance to support you by listening well.*

Spirit communicates with us, gently at first, tugging on our clothing like a toddler seeking our attention. Without a response, Spirit increases the volume until an all-out tantrum forces us into acute awareness.

Spirit guides us in positive, uplifting directions and continually has our highest good at heart. Give Spirit the best chance to support you by listening well.

Try This:

1. Begin noticing where and when you are most able to listen to yourself. What are your ideal circumstances? How can you go about deliberately creating listening opportunities? Journal about what you've discovered. In the beginning, your inner listening might sound an awful lot like a to-do list. Keep going. Remember, by collecting your concerns and action items into one place, you are making space to hear what your heart most wants to tell you.

2. Set aside a listening time and place that works best for you. Make use of it at least once each day. On exceptionally hectic days, I use the time in the car as my quiet space. For the first ten minutes of any trip, I don't listen to music, affirmations or anything else. I don't answer my phone or use social media. There are days when the conversations I'm having with myself are so interesting that I forget to turn anything on. At home, that time is often in bed, at the very end of the day, in the twilight before sleep. We all have a rich inner life where the one we call Spirit has much insight to share.

3. For the next week, at the end of each day, record what you heard when you listened to yourself. These insights are treasures. Treat them with the respect they deserve. While what you heard might not be something you're willing to act on immediately, capture it to ponder in the days ahead.

4. Honor what you hear. What value does the input have in your life? How might you pay attention? What about the information you receive feels true to you? When my inner voice speaks, the words strongly resonate with me. I've learned to listen and act.

Be Willing to Be Uncomfortable

It's good to do uncomfortable things. It's weight training for life.

—Anne Lamott

Dear You,

You may not know what you are going to do once you get there. That's acceptable. You know you are ultimately going to get there and at times that has to be adequate. Sometimes the only "doing" or planning that is required is being willing to show up. Showing up, in spite of uncertainty or discomfort, is an act of love. It takes a lot of confidence to begin a journey without a clear route. I have noticed that all of that pre-planning and advance routing work often acts as a substitute for actually getting started packing for your journey.

I heard a clarity ninja named Caren Albers assure her friend, "There are no wrong turns." I laughed when I heard her say it, because I am known to swing into a wrong turn or two.

There's the whole thing of proximal direction. A fancy term which means that as long as you are heading in the approximately correct direction, you can take every next step with a degree of confidence. Caren's assurance is especially true when you are facing the general direction of your dreams. Even when you are marching steadfastly in an opposite direction it's not really a wrong turn—just a more scenic route. Some of the "worst" turns of my life have ultimately landed me where I needed to be. My best blessing for a journey taker is, "May every road lead you home."

Now, stop speculating on the route, get packing and get going.

Love,

Your Life

Most of us don't begin the day by enthusiastically thinking, "Oh! I hope I get to be uncomfortable all day long." Those days come, on their own, without invitation. A willingness to be uncomfortable is a profound RSVP to life's invitation to change.

That feeling of awkwardness is a sure sign that something is on the cusp of being learned, changed or challenged. In any of those events there is an opportunity to grow, to become stronger. There are those people, and perhaps you are one of them, whose primary objective in creating plans is to remain at ease. Comfortable. Unshaken. That can create a sense of calm and order, which contributes to an enjoyable experience both for the planner and those for whom the plan is established.

The willingness to be uncomfortable is a signal to the universe that you are open, willing to see something that has been familiar in a new way. It indicates you see the possibility that the way you have always done a thing may need or benefit from a fresh approach.

People often refer to chasing a new, chaotic or random idea as "going down the rabbit hole." As Alice slipped from what she knew to a whole new world of wonder, I am quite certain the child traveling through a wee rabbit hole experienced some actual discomfort. The account of everything that happened after the discomfort makes it all seem worth the squeeze.

Periodically, just to stay on my toes, I require myself to observe the things to which I am experiencing resistance. Sometimes I make a list and systematically look at my resistance and ask myself to participate in some or all of that thing. Other times, once I notice the impulse to push away from something, I'll ask myself to move toward instead of away. Sometimes resistance masquerades as procrastination and that is a good thing to get closer to! Being willing to be uncomfortable requires me to be observant of that which is causing me discomfort. Context is important to note in this. As a child, discomfort was often the precursor to amazing and memorable adventures.

Then, I grew up. I wanted answers, explanations, order and control. I wanted to know where I was going and how I was going to get there. I thought planning and organizing and KNOWING the answers to both the obvious and the anticipated was the key to success. I wonder how many miracles and gifts I inadvertently passed up when I was on that road of comfortable control.

Discomfort can be read several different ways. Sometimes discomfort is intuition knocking gently on your door with a warning or sense of caution. Being uncomfortable happens in discovery, in opposition, in process of all kinds. It happens in the part where the first steps have been taken and your inside-the-head voice is shouting, *What's next?* and the very disconcerting answer is, *I don't know*. When you lovingly listen to yourself, you begin to know the difference between those two kinds of uncomfortableness.

Try This:

1. Examine your relationship to discomfort. As you contemplate the potential for discomfort in a situation that is new to you, consider remembering Alice and all the wonder that came after the discomfort.
2. Reframe discomfort. It's not possible to know what you don't know! Moving forward into something that creates discomfort is an opportunity to learn. Either there will be discovery or affirmation. You'll be surprised at learning something unexpected or you will underscore that there was a good reason for the discomfort and that's the end of that!
3. Read Rilke's *Letters to a Young Poet* (or re-read). Pay special attention to the "learn to love the questions themselves" part.
4. Notice the difference in how you feel when you remain curious and when you attempt to exert control.

Slow Down to Show Up

There is more to life than increasing its speed.

—*Mahatma Gandhi*

Dear You,

The needs of the world are more than one person can address. However, the needs of one person make it possible to do something towards improving the experience of another. Maybe you can't give someone a home, but perhaps you can give them a coat, or the dignity of a greeting and a smile. It is a natural impulse to want to alleviate someone's sorrow, to make them feel better. That feels better for you, too.

In the face of fresh loss, a different impulse is called to service. See the grief. Sit beside it and know that sorrow has a season. Your greatest gesture can be to do nothing beyond this: Slow down, sit and stay. Regardless of the size of an action, the most important thing is that when you see something you are able to do, you do it.

Love,

Your Life

We can find ourselves on the fast track without realizing how we got there. Too frequently Pam and I react as if every invitation and communication is urgent. One afternoon we received a text from a friend asking if we were in town and if so, could we stop over in a couple of hours to visit their son, just home from overseas. My first thought was, *We've got to see him, so there goes our afternoon of writing, work and cooking—at our pace.* Then I took a breath, paused and examined my response. Was this an emergency or was I creating one? I texted back, "How long is Justin home for?" "Two weeks," came the response. I breathed again, this time with relief as I assured her that we would visit him but not today.

When you spend enough time racing from one activity and emergency to another, everything begins to take on the same sense of urgency—regardless of its true nature. By honoring our need to be home, I eased Pam's mind and mine. Some days, we use a numerical scale asking, "How important is this on a scale of one to ten?" Everything can't be a ten.

When an ambulance rushed my dad, completely unresponsive, to the hospital, I received my master's degree in slowing down. Nothing mattered except what was happening in the emergency room and later, intensive care. Suddenly I had a new measuring stick. Is someone dying? If not, can this wait?

Each of our clients completely understood where they stood in our priorities at the moment. Some things went on the back burner; some fell off the stove. Slowing down allowed us to be completely present with Dad, Mom and my siblings. Slowing down allowed us to notify relatives, pray, cry, hold one another and gently say goodbye over the next two days as Dad's heart slowly gave out.

> *Slowing down allows you to respond rather than react to life as you move through it.*

Slowing down allows us to prioritize, to discover what matters in the world and choose accordingly. Without taking time-outs, without examining our own responses moment by moment, we tend to only the urgent and miss out on what is truly important.

Slowing down allows you to respond rather than react to life as you move through it.

Mary Anne is keen to comment on the contradiction of this idea:

It's counterintuitive, at first glance, to consider the advice to slow down in order to show up. The inclination, when someone in our peer circle or family has pressing needs, is to speed up. The impulse to go faster stems from believing everything that was planned before the event must be completed. It is assumed that increasing the velocity of your actions will allow you to add the opportunity to show up for someone you care about. When additional requirements are added to the day, slow down, assess, reprioritize, reassign. Consider the all of your everything so you can make the best decision for yourself and others. This may involve choosing to set aside or eliminate something that previously seemed important.

Over time you may have noticed that pressured, unthinking speeding up makes accidents and missteps more likely. Bumps and bruises often accompany me on the rushing journey! Mindfulness can indeed involve speed but it rarely involves rush. Speed is the hallmark of a skilled athlete. When the thoughtful balance of weighing known and unexpected things is present, you get to be surprised by how much you can actually accomplish, along with purposeful direction. Keep on with the practice of slowing down so that the best parts of yourself show up for you in self-care and in caring for others.

Try This:

1. Create your own priority scale and check in with yourself on a regular basis. Practice using it during this week. Note your experiences in your journal.

2. Before automatically answering yes when asked to add something to your calendar, practice asking yourself, *If I say yes to this, what am I saying no to?* How does this impact your response?

3. Give yourself permission to ask, "Can I get back with you tomorrow?" It is okay to put thought into deciding how to use your time. What did you notice when you practiced this?

4. Set aside time in your calendar for you, not for any specific activity. Begin to practice slowing down. A friend of mine used to say, "Coaching is deliberate life change—without the heart attack." It took the experience with my dad to fully understand that. As with any change, slowing down is a practice. Begin today—and keep practicing.

Chapter Two: Clean House

The more anger towards the past you carry in your heart,
the less capable you are for loving in the present.

—*Barbara de Angelis*

Dear You,

Feng Shui (that ancient art of space balancing)
isn't just a principle for your physical environment.
There is a system of balance and beauty, unique to
you, that is directed by the compass of your heart.
That internal space often impacts how your outward
environment looks and feels. It's like a system of
metaphysical mirrors—each reflects the other.

And, about that balance thing. You can have the
most orderly, clean, living environment imaginable
and have crushing chaos swirling on the inside. It's
quite a contradiction. It's sounds kind of funny—
but it's true—balance on the outside is an inside job!
And balance on the inside can be led by what is on
the outside.

Gently, let me ask, "Is it time to clean house?"

Love,

Your Life

One of the most impactful ways to show up with love for yourself involves cleaning your physical and emotional house. Sometimes cleaning house means just that.

Outwardly my life looked nearly perfect. My partner and I had impressive jobs and a tight circle of longtime friends. Our finances were secure. We'd just purchased our dream home, a last-ditch effort to patch over the deep ache of loneliness that no one suspected. I had everything I wanted except the love and intimacy I craved. I'd even convinced myself that settling for less worked—until my Mom's breast cancer diagnosis jolted me awake.

This time, instead of looking outward for answers, I mined the dozens of boxes I'd accumulated and carted from one place to another since my college years for clues. By fearlessly examining their contents, noting patterns and letting go of most everything, I reconnected with the adventurous, generous, loving woman I'd almost buried. It was the courageous first step towards rebirth. Within eighteen months, I was in the relationship of my dreams. Without letting go, I'd never have had room for the love of a lifetime.

Other times, the cleaning reaches even deeper. My former minister, Joyce Stone, once unforgettably demonstrated this. That Sunday, unlike most, Joyce started her sermon in silence at the back of the church, dragging and carrying as many types of luggage as her hands, arms, shoulders, and back could bear.

As she slowly worked her way down the aisle, the collected weight and size of the bags almost prohibited any forward momentum. When she did walk, the largest bags swayed precariously from side to side, brushing and in some cases, striking those seated in the pews. To keep the bags from getting stuck, Joyce juggled, pulled, shoved and twisted them, continually readjusting the various straps for maximum hold. Congregants ducked and scooted away from the aisle seats, avoiding what would have been painful contact. As Joyce moved down the aisle, she hurt others. Each step required enormous amounts of energy until she finally released the bags.

Emotional baggage is heavy, hurtful and draining. Holding on serves no purpose other than to keep us from living and loving fully in the present. Holding onto emotional baggage creates barriers between ourselves and others. Not surprisingly, her sermon that day was about letting go.

> Holding on serves no purpose other than to keep us from living and loving fully in the present.

How can we possibly fully travel with another when our own journey suffers from baggage overload? How can we reach out in love when our arms are already full? How can we open our hearts to love if we've put them on lockdown?

We can either fight our way through life clinging to every hurt and every "who done us wrong" or lighten our load by regularly cleaning house.

Isn't it time to let go?

Try This:

1. Think of cleaning up your emotional space like you do your physical space. What "piles" do you have sitting around? What has been taking up emotional space in your life? What are you ready to let go of? Make note of these in your journal.

2. What baggage keeps you from living the life of your dreams? Your baggage can be physical items, memories, limiting beliefs or something else. What steps are you willing to take in order to clean house? Take one action today. Share your success with a friend, identify your next step and plan time for it.

3. Notice when you find yourself having "everything but the kitchen sink" conversations—that is, even though something minimal may have occurred between you and another person, you drag every wrongdoing you've ever experienced with them into the present conversation. What are you upset about in the moment and what is in the bag you've been carting around for years? If you need to step away from the conversation to think, ask for a time-out. If necessary, ask for an extended time-out. Identify what you need to say lovingly and what you want to let go of. Have the conversations. If necessary, practice with a friend or therapist beforehand.

4. Begin communicating courageously in the present. Commit to continually improving your communication skills. You will spend less time cleaning house later on by your willingness to express yourself and ask for what you need in a manner others can now hear.

Forgive Yourself

Be gentle first with yourself.

—*Lama Yeshe*

Dear You,

I plan on sending you the universal equivalent of flowers today in order to distract you from the harshness you extend to yourself. If I spoke to you in the manner that you address yourself—constantly— you might be a continuous puddle of tears. Or, at least, sad a good deal of the time. Since time as you know it is linear, there's no changing what you did. Forgiving yourself opens the road to change what you could do. The "do" or not yet "DOne" is something you are still in charge of.

Please stop looking in the rearview mirror of the vehicle that is your life. Face forward. Forgive and get yourself out of reverse and in gear to move forward. The very same event can look like an ending or beginning: It all depends on whether you are looking back or straight ahead. Which way will you choose to look?

Also, while you are looking, be on the lookout for something that feels a lot like a bouquet of flowers today.

Love,

Your Life

Why do we often find it easier to forgive others than to forgive ourselves? After wrapping up a relationship class for singles, a student approached and introduced herself, quickly confiding that she'd completely blown her last relationship. From her words, I got the impression she'd cheated on her partner. She went on for another half hour berating herself for missing out on the chance to continue the relationship of her dreams. When she finally drew a breath, I asked, "How long ago was this?"

"Thirty years."

Her response stunned me.

For thirty years she'd tortured herself for a mistake made early on. For thirty years she'd deprived herself of the joy of another long-term relationship because she couldn't let go of the one who got away. I urged her to seek counseling to forgive herself and move on with life and love.

Compare that with Sandra's experience.

Sandra thought she did the right thing. After her divorce, she waited until her elementary age children finished college before dating again. She used an online dating service but quickly grew disheartened by the men she met. Finally, after more than a dozen first dates, Sandra met a man who dazzled her with his intellect, sharp wit and shared passion for football.

With Eric, Sandra felt like a princess. He bought her gifts, called frequently and doted on her—something no man had ever done. He was well-educated with an impressive job and a large extended family with whom Sandra quickly fell in love. After three short months, they set a wedding date. Within days Sandra felt confused, ambivalent—afraid even. She began noticing hints of a temper. Rather than trusting her gut and walking away, she walked down the aisle with Eric by her side.

The relationship quickly deteriorated. Mr. Perfect grew demanding. Nothing was good enough. When angry, he threw tantrums and eventually, objects. He continually checked up on her. For three suffocating years, Sandra stayed, wondering if she was responsible for his anger. When she found the courage to leave, it took months to realize his rage wasn't her fault and to let herself off the hook for marrying the man who initially resembled Prince Charming.

She spent the first few months berating herself for ignoring the signs during their courtship and a few more for not leaving sooner. Ultimately, after researching more about the deceptive dating practices of abusers, she forgave herself. She realized that Eric took advantage of her insecurities. Once Sandra offered herself the gift of forgiveness, her laughter, courage and self-confidence returned.

Without practice, self-forgiveness can feel daunting. Sometimes it is easier to forgive others than ourselves. We tend to be more understanding, gentle and loving with friends and family. Starting today, use that same loving forgiveness with yourself. You deserve it.

Try This:

1. On a blank sheet of paper, write these words across the top: "I forgive myself for..." then fill up the page. If necessary, turn the page over and keep going. Make a list of anything you haven't forgiven yourself for. Keep writing until you can't think of another thing; then look at yourself through the eyes of love.
2. Remind yourself that you made the best possible choices with the information you had available at the time. Tell yourself, It's okay to move on; it's okay to forgive myself. Today is a new day. When you are ready, let the list go for good. Tear it up. If you decide to burn your list. choose a very safe place with something to douse the flames nearby.
3. Notice the tone and words you use when self-correcting. If they are not kind, give yourself a do-over. Speak to yourself the way you would a dear friend who had done the same thing.
4. Consider counseling if you find self-forgiveness challenging.

Forgive Others

Forgiveness does not change the past, but
it does enlarge the future.

—*Paul Boese*

Dear You,

Let me get right to the point.

You are not in charge of anyone but you. You have been wronged. You have been treated poorly. I concur. And here's what I have to say about it:

Forgive them. To hold the event without forgiveness is to allow the wrong to occur repeatedly. You were hurt once by an outside force. And then look what happened—by reliving the hurt, by not letting it go and forgiving the instance, you hurt yourself so many more times.

Even if you are tempted to believe they do not deserve forgiveness, remember, you do not forgive them for their sake. It is for your own. YOU deserve to forgive. So please, stop repeating the harm. You did not deserve to be treated that way then, and you do not deserve to treat yourself to the continual misfortune now.

Love,

Your Life

Pam's dad officially adopted her as his own when she was just three years old, right after he married her mom. He was the only dad she had ever known until her eleventh birthday when her parents sat her down and explained how he came to adopt her.

"This doesn't change anything," her dad said, tears streaming down his face. "You are and always will be my little girl." It was an emotional time for the entire family.

From then on, Pam wondered about the man who chose to give her up, who abandoned her for a different life. She gleaned pieces of the story and understood she'd been erased from his life with a single signature from the man who would have been her grandfather. She became another long-buried secret common to small Southern towns.

As her sixteenth birthday approached, she asked her mother for permission to meet her biological father but instead received a pair of red shoes. What her parents didn't mention was that her biological father declined. Out of love, her parents absorbed the full brunt of her disappointment.

Pam remained curious about her birth father, learned his name and where he lived, yet she did nothing with the information for another sixteen years. In her early thirties, Pam finally made the call. But before that day arrived, before she ever picked up the phone, she readied her heart. She forgave the man who gave her up before she was even born. She let go of tightly held resentments and any expectations of what might come out of the call.

"Jimmy? It's me, Pam—your daughter."

There wasn't a single breath of silence between her words and his.

"I've been expecting your call."

They talked for hours that night. Pam got off the call, not with all the answers she was looking for, but with a better understanding of the man who'd let her go. They soon met in person and from that point on, Jimmy called every Sunday night, always expressing pride in the woman she'd become.

Less than a year later, Pam received a surprise call from Jimmy's son, her half-brother, and learned that Jimmy was hospitalized with a brain aneurysm.

During her first visit to see Jimmy in the hospital, a nurse asked Pam if she wanted to rub lotion on Jimmy's skin to make him more comfortable. Though he could no longer speak, when their eyes met, his almost imperceptible nod let her know it would be okay.

Then this young woman, who at one point felt utterly abandoned by this man, warmed the lotion in her hands and spent the next half hour gently rubbing it onto his skin. Anything that came before that moment melted. She was a girl, unconditionally loving the man who gave her life, giving him something he'd never been able to do for her. I'm sure his heart ached for keeping Pam at such a distance for much of his life. I'm sure he knew then what a beautiful, loving human he'd brought into the world. If she were his only legacy, the world was already a better place. He died just six months later.

> **❝** *Forgiveness frees your heart, instantly expanding its capacity to love.*

Pam's willingness to forgive birthed both a hoped for reconciliation and a surprise bonus family who openly welcomed us both. Forgiveness frees your heart, instantly expanding its capacity to love.

Try This:

1. When someone annoys you today, instead of stuffing it inside, pause. See the other person as doing the very best they can in that moment. Remind yourself that their actions are not about you. I internally say, *I forgive you,* then let it go. Ask yourself what you are willing to do to make forgiveness a part your daily practice.
2. Think of someone you've been unable to forgive. Ask yourself how not forgiving this person serves you.
3. Forgiveness is an inside job. Think of someone you're unable to forgive. Take out a piece of paper and at the top write, I forgive (insert their name) for... and then list all of the things you forgive the person for including any perceived slights or injustices. Put it all out there in one place. Keep going until you've run out of things to forgive. Read it over. Breathe. Let it go. When you are ready, destroy the list.
4. If, after practicing forgiveness, you still find yourself unable to forgive someone, find a counselor to help you move forward successfully.

The Art of the Reframe

One sees great things from the valley;
only small things from the peak.

—C.K. Chesterton

Dear You,

Allow yourself to be defined as much by what you are as what you are not. The road you have taken is informed by the many paths you did not choose. At the end of the day, reflect on all you did accomplish as well as notice what you did not get done. Tomorrow offers a fresh, and different, kind of opportunity. Start a new list.

A practical way to utilize a reframing mentality works wonders. Instead of bemoaning that you only half-finished what you had intended, you can celebrate that TODAY you finished Part One. Tomorrow you get to tackle Part Two. See what I did there? Not only does it sound better, it's absolutely true! And it feels better, too. Try it.

Every big thing is made up of incremental tasks— celebrate your small successes every chance you get.

Love,

Your Life

Pam and I signed up for a seven-day, 350-mile bike ride in north Florida. After putting in an unexpectedly hilly 50 miles on the first day, we waited in long lines for dinner, bathrooms, and later, showers. I recall thinking this wasn't exactly what I thought it would be like. I felt myself becoming grumpy. We walked to the back of the building to eat in silence. After settling onto the concrete, we looked at one another. Pam said, "Well, we're not in Kansas anymore." "No," I replied, "so welcome to Planet Bike." Instantly we both put aside all preconceived notions of what the trip would be like and let every day be a welcome surprise.

With that, we reframed our entire outlook on the experience. Food would be whatever was served us, and it would taste good. Wherever we put our head down would be fine. Whether our route was hilly, flat or some combination, we would finish it, grateful for the experience. Whatever the weather, it was part of the adventure—adding to the stories we would retell for years to come. And we had it all: cold showers, long lines, flat tires, ferocious headwinds plus pouring rain. But because we'd reframed early on, we'd turn to each other, smile and say "Planet Bike."

One of my takeaways from an evening spent listening to Bert Jacobs, co-founder of Life is Good,™ was that no one in their company uses the words "have to" about any job they take on. They use "get to." Mary Anne loves to observe that just one "E" makes a big difference - gEt to or got to. I get to take out the garbage. I get to make 40 phone calls today. See the difference? It's all in the reframe.

I could be angry about having many thousands of dollars in student loan debt upon graduation because my parents were unable to assist any of us with college expenses. Instead, I choose to focus on what my parents did. They gave my four siblings and me a childhood full of richness money can't buy. Today, three of us live in the same town as our Mom. We see each other regularly, hang out, stay connected with the nephews and are enmeshed in each other's lives—in a good way.

My parents allowed us to be children. They lovingly kept grownup discussions behind closed doors. Although I later learned we were quite poor, I never noticed. Our household overflowed with enough

> *Reframing is a gift you give yourself and others. You choose what you focus on. The type of frame doesn't matter; what you display inside and carry in your heart does.*

love to support the seven of us plus scores of friends who chose to call our house their second home. Mom kept a steady supply of Kool-Aid™ on hand. When one pitcher ran low, she'd add the next flavor, calling it dragon juice. We drank it up.

Reframing is a gift you give yourself and others. You choose what you focus on. The type of frame doesn't matter; what you display inside and carry in your heart does. Which would you rather have on your wall: a picture of your student loan balance at the end of college or a collage of photos full of family experiences? I paid off my college debt years ago. The connection to my family continues to pay rich dividends many years after we first raised cups of dragon juice in celebration of another fine summer day.

Try This:

1. Reflect on how the practice of reframing situations or memories could positively impact your life. Record your thoughts before moving on.
2. Pick one memory you'd like to reframe. Using the above examples, consider how you might choose to do so.
3. Choose a current situation to reframe. Example: This week I'm working on the book you hold in your hands. Part of me is terrified. Another part is excited beyond belief. I choose to see this as one of the most exciting times of my life.
4. Begin to see yourself as a re-framer in real time. Perhaps you are familiar with the expression, "The present is perfect." When you find yourself fuming about sitting in traffic, ask what's perfect about this situation. Reframe in the moment. Try, "Wow, it's not often I get the chance to take a breath" or "The universe/ God must be protecting me in some way." Or simply notice and appreciate your surroundings.

Chapter Three:
Stand Up For Yourself

Stand up for yourself by not standing yourself up.

—Gina Greenlee

Dear You,

Do not be fooled by the dazzling, the daring, the Do It Now While This Special Offer Lasts. Do not be fooled by celebrity, notoriety and collecting LIKES the way you collected pennies when you were a kid. Do not be conned by comparison, condescension or catwalks.

There is hate in the world: Stand up for your friend. There is war: Hold your tongue and reach for grace. There is illness: Practice self-care so you can best care for others. You can address The Big by taking measurable action in The Small.

The extraordinary will always entice. Today remember and do what matters to you. The next most important thing on your list. Due diligence in your day serves a greater good in the world. Not all are called to run into burning buildings to save a life. You can turn to the burning passion in your own soul and save your Own Life. It is then, from your own fullness, from standing up for yourself, that you have the strength and motivation to stand up for others.

Love,

Your Life

I frequently remind coaching clients that they are high performance vehicles, not everyday cars; they can't treat themselves poorly yet still expect top-level performance. Neither can you. We often put work, family, social obligations and everything else first—until a significant life event, such as cancer or the death of a loved one, quickly reorders priorities moving self-care closer to number one.

I'm all about prevention and a huge part of prevention is maintenance. We drive an 11 year old car with just over 150,000 miles on the odometer. It runs like a dream because we maintain it meticulously. It goes to the dealership more often than I visit the doctor. I'm on a first name basis with my service advisor. We both envision the car running perfectly at 300,000 miles. At the rate we are going, that's another eleven years. There's only one way that will happen: maintenance and TLC (tender loving care).

My mechanic uses genuine manufacturer's parts, even for the oil change. He uses a high grade of engine oil. I'm picky about what goes into the car and who works on the car. Can you say the same about yourself? If you set that same intention for yourself, how might you treat yourself differently? And what would excellent maintenance look like?

No one will make your health and well-being a priority, except you. You will always be asked for more than you can give.

Standing up for yourself means exercising your "no" and your "yes," as well as your body. It means getting enough rest and planning recharge time as solidly as you block out time to attend your daughter's soccer game or nephew's piano recital. Many of us automatically say yes when asked for commitments of our time then wonder why we're tired by three in the afternoon. We definitely need to make appointments—with ourselves. When was the last time you blocked time off on your calendar to make room for you? When was the last time you nurtured you? When was the last time you made time for fun?

You are in charge of you. Stand up for yourself just as much as you would stand up for someone you dearly love.

If a dear friend's schedule was too packed, what advice would you give them?

If a loved one said the doctor suggested that they had a high risk of diabetes, heart attack or stroke, what advice would you give them?

If someone looked utterly worn out day after day, what advice might you offer?

> *Sometimes the simplest love letter to yourself reads "Yes."*

You are smart, strong, intelligent, generous and loving. You'll offer a stranger the shirt off your back. You'll stay late at work. How will you show up for yourself? Where will you draw a line in the sand on behalf of your own interest? What will your stand look like?

Sometimes the simplest love letter to yourself reads "Yes."

Try This:

1. Think of one area in your life where you've already successfully taken a stand around your own well-being. What stand have you taken and how has it served you? What allowed you to be successful? How will you use this strength as you begin to take other stands for yourself? Journal about this.
2. Identify one area where you are willing to take a stand for yourself. Write it down. Then list at least three baby steps toward making this change. Take the first one today.
3. Interview a friend who excels at standing up for themselves. Ask them what gives them the courage to do so on a regular basis.
4. Think of yourself as one of your finest friends. Stand up for yourself with the same practiced ease that you would use on behalf of a dear friend.

Nurture Yourself

Nurture yourself and allow others to nurture you.

—The Circle of Nurture

Dear You,

You've been hearing the Do-It-Yourself, Pull Yourself Up By Your Bootstraps philosophy since you were tiny. Those bootstraps are essential metaphors for independence and self-reliance. The pendulum also swings to the equally necessary interdependence.

Forget that bootstrap philosophy for just a bit. Let me remind you of the care and feeding instructions I sent with you. (Oh my, did you lose them?) Pay attention to the ways your body tells you it is overtaxed. **Before** you receive the overtaxed message is a good time to ask for help, assistance, mutual participation. Just because you can do something all by yourself does not mean it is in your best interest to go it alone. When you teach yourself the art of self-care (good rest, nurturing food, positive movement, meaningful activity) it becomes much easier to accept nurturing from others. It's a dynamic circle.

So. Whisper these words to yourself, "Rest. RESTore. Invite. Embrace. Accept." You'll get it done—and about that accepting the offer of help? Remember, a thing is more fun when you get it done together.

Love,

Your Life

We all need nurturing. On an extended work project in Virginia, Pam and I had worked for three straight weeks and desperately needed some R&R—rest and relaxation. Already exhausted, we spent the first day of our only free weekend running my college-age nephew to the doctor and making sure he was on the mend. We'd committed to a dinner party that evening but intuitively knew hours spent making small talk with strangers would leave us drained and ill-prepared for the demanding week ahead. Pam called our hosts and bowed out, a small but necessary act of self-nurturing.

Running full steam ahead without recharging our own batteries is the perfect recipe for a physical or emotional meltdown, yet self-nurturing doesn't come easily to many of us. We give until we're running on empty, but refuse to refill our tanks. As grownups, we must call a time-out for self-care.

Nurturing yourself means anything from deep breathing to massages to a two-week transatlantic cruise where the only thing on your agenda is staring out over the ocean. You choose what works in your situation.

Since many of us don't have a personal masseuse on speed dial, the ability to self-nurture is paramount. Your choice depends on your circumstances in the moment. I hear the reasons you can't stop to nurture yourself: I'm a caregiver for an aging parent. I'm working two jobs to make ends meet. I can't take one night off, much less take a vacation. I've got four children and no family nearby to help. Even in those situations, you can self-nurture: Listen to soothing music, step outside and look at the night sky or take a walk around the block, stretch, or practice deep breathing. It's a start. More flexibility could mean a yoga class, a night out with friends, or a short getaway.

Personally, I love Pajama Days complete with my favorite teas or coffees, healthy finger foods, a great book, an extended soak in the tub and a nap. I also enjoy time spent in nature, with friends, and on spontaneous adventures.

And when our schedules heat up, we call in the troops for help with errands, grocery shopping and food prep.

As crucial as self-nurturing is, allowing others to nurture us is equally important. That night in Virginia, we both had the chance to practice.

Our hosts, also our temporary landlords, understood. Throughout the evening, they tapped on the door leading to our basement apartment with brief announcements: "Here's an extra casserole dish of vegetable lasagna. All you need to do is heat it up in the microwave." Or "The salad is ready if you want to come fix yourself a bowl." Or "There are some really great side dishes, if you want to come into the kitchen and fill your plate."

At the end, there was one more tap on the door. Bruce handed me two slices of what he described as "the best carrot cake this side of heaven." As a lifelong carrot cake aficionado, I can attest to the truth in those words.

> *Nurture yourself but be willing to ask for nurturing, too.*

We felt loved, pampered and nurtured. Our sweet friends honored our need for a time-out yet still found ways to deeply care for us. And we were smart enough to accept their care.

Nurture yourself but be willing to ask for nurturing, too.

Try This:

1. Practice noticing when you need nurturing. Connect with yourself. How does the need for self-nurturing manifest itself in your life? What happens when you don't pay attention to the first clue? Journal about this. Example: I get tense and if I ignore that, I get grouchy and if I ignore that, I don't even want to be in my own company! What nurtures you more than anything? Find ways to give yourself that which most nurtures you.

2. Select three brief self-nurturing practices and incorporate each one at least once into your day. Think of this as the start of your weekday prescription for restoration. ℞: For the next five days, sprinkle three brief nurturing habits throughout each day. Journal about your experience with this intentional practice. Add one longer self-nurturing practice to your day at least twice this week.

3. Practice letting others nurture you. The next time someone offers to help you, say yes.

4. Tell others how they can nurture you. This is a biggie. It takes courage and a bit of vulnerability. Pam asks for pedicure gift certificates. She asks me to rub her shoulders. I let people know when I need silence. Yes, sometimes the gift of silence feels nurturing to me. How will others know if you don't tell them?

Take Care of Your Health

To keep the body in good health is a duty... otherwise we shall not be able to keep our mind strong and clear.

—Buddha

Dear You,

You might have an external hard drive for that computer of yours... but there's no external hard drive for you! And as hard as you drive yourself, it would be great if there was! I know that you have a lot of stuff to do. Here's what I know about that: You'll probably **always** have a lot of stuff to do. It seems to be the way of the world. It's kind of an irony that by choosing to often do nothing... you get more done.

Look around.... the natural world shows you the way. Flowers do not bloom 24/7/365. They have cycles. And there's the whole season thing. You get my point. There's nobody who has a greater interest in your taking care of your health than me! Your life. We're kind of in this dance together. C'mon partner. The first and most important stuff to do are the things that are going to elevate your wellness... for the long haul. Let's do this!

Love,

Your Life

Mary Anne shares some thoughts on taking care of your health:

Imagine. There's only one road, one path to your home. The home you own and the only place you have to live. I feel confident you would take fine care of that road. You would make sure it would accommodate you and your travels in all seasons, in any kind of weather. Because... It's your home! All the things you own are likely in that one spot. It's where you eat and entertain and rest and play. This may strike you as obvious. Wouldn't anyone want to have unfettered access, easy approach, to their own home? You would think so, wouldn't you?

Our body is the home in which we house our life force, our thoughts, our dreams. It's where we generate our ideas and how we extend compassion and service to the world. And the route we travel to maintaining that dwelling can be pretty rough. It's easy to succumb to the pressure of overtime, of constant activity, mindless eating, cutting sleep short in favor of so many other choices. I've said it myself, "I can sleep when I'm dead!"And I spent my teenage years staring at a poster on my bedroom wall, "I'd rather wear out than rust out." Now I know there are a lot more choices. Sleep is the fuel that keeps me going with consistency. Hydration helps sustain the function of my body much the same as high quality fuel keeps a vehicle going. While the diet experts would like you to believe that their specific plan is the best for you, it's most likely that you know what is best for you and your body.

I remember the time I asked a respected poet of some reputation for his best writing advice. The two things that he said really surprised me. He told me to take care of my teeth and to tend my knees. I laughed, at first. I thought he was kidding with me. I clarified that I'd asked him for his best writing advice. He assured me that's what he had given me. He explained that if I wanted to be a good writer, I had to take care of my health. If I was fit and strong, my writing would occur from that place of health. My once-in-a-lifetime-dog, Judah, demonstrated some similar advice. If he could have put words to what he demonstrated, it would have been, "When you are tired of turning in circles, chasing your tail, stop. Sit down. Rest." Good dog!

Try This:

1. Keep a health log for three months in a row. Observe your habits and patterns. Learn when you are most energetic in the day. Note what you eat and how it makes you feel. By noticing these patterns over a 90 day period, you can determine foods and activities that both drain you and energize you.

2. You block off time in your calendar for commitments to others. Do the same for yourself.

3. Stop before you get too tired to think. Learn to notice the signs that you are pushing too hard and stop yourself, before your body does the stopping for you.

4. Make more time in your weekly plan for the things that energize you and make you feel better and stronger. When you are your best self you are able to offer your best efforts to the things that matter most to you.

Make Time for Fun

Fun is good.

—Dr. Seuss

Dear You,

In the cycle of 24-hour news and what can feel like increasing demands on your time, "Have fun" may seem like frivolous advice. The opposite is actually correct and finally scientists and neurologists are catching on. Fun is essential to physical and mental health. It is a natural antidote to stress. I know you've heard, "Laughter is the best medicine." Yes. And fun! They kind of go together, don't you think? Fun is a wellspring of fresh thinking and new ideas. Fun is the restart button when you've run out of good solutions to a problem.

Need proof? Next time you are growling and just about ready to lose your temper because you can't figure something out, make time for fun. I feel confident you will return to the task and find a fairly decent solution, one that will have you wondering how you managed to miss it before. Fun. It's what smart people are doing in between being so busy!

Now, go practice being a better thinker and problem solver by making time for fun. (I'm serious!)

Love,

Your Life

Does it ever feel as if you've become a little too grown up? You've got a mortgage, a job, kids, aging parents, you've taken on volunteer activities, signed up for yoga and manage the family finances. You're loaded with responsibilities. As adults, we're often spectators, watching others have fun while forgetting to have some of our own. You require restoration. I encourage you to deliberately include fun as part of the process.

Sometimes fun leaps into our lives, unexpectedly; other times we must seek it out. Pam and I once attended a free Kool and the Gang concert when it would have been easier to stay home. Storm clouds threatened and traffic guaranteed to be challenging. Indeed, traffic crawled but not as much as I'd imagined before leaving home. We showed up and it poured. The best part? When the band belted out *Celebration*, we danced in the rain along with a few thousand other brave souls. After all, who can resist dancing to *Celebration*, rain or no rain?

As adults, don't we do our best to avoid getting rained on? Don't we typically have umbrellas and ponchos at the ready? But umbrellas had no place in the park. Along with other concertgoers, we relived childhood—as adults, making memories we'd carry forward like souvenirs, bringing us back to the sweet moment when we collectively said, "What the heck" and danced. Not caring we'd get our car seats wet, not caring we'd be soaked for at least another hour, not caring about the potential consequences. This choice was about living all out, in the moment. It was about showing up for fun.

When we spent two years as emotional caregivers to my older brother, our nephews made certain we made time for fun. During our free moments, they invited us to the movies or over to their house where we spent hours playing games. They kept us entertained with a steady stream of jokes they found online and introduced us to clean comedians on social media.

Working on a monumental project, doing my best to meet a deadline, while sweating over complexities and details, my sister-in-law texted, "Any interest in seeing a movie with us?" I read the message to Pam and looked for her reaction. She nodded, adding, "If you're in, I'm in." I texted back, "We'd love to join you. When?" It turned out the movie started in twenty minutes.

We raced around the house like madwomen mainlining adrenaline and made it to the theater just in time for summer previews. As the lights dimmed, my brother slipped his hand into our shared popcorn. Everything felt right with the world. The film was funnier than I expected and we belly laughed until the credits began rolling—just what the doctor ordered. That night as I prepared for bed, my brain raced with ideas. While I slept, solutions danced in my dreams. I awoke refreshed, with renewed energy and enthusiasm for the task at hand.

Whatever fun looks like for you, make time for it. Fun nourishes and restores you, snaps you out of the day-to-day, and readies you for life's surprises. Know your fun quota and plan to meet it regularly.

Try This:

1. Set aside at least fifteen minutes for fun, even on the busiest of days. A friend introduced us to the game Bananagrams. Even when we can't play an entire game, we use it as a fun break between projects. How might you find your daily fun? Come up with at least three different ideas and try them this week.

2. Explore your fun options for the weekend. In most cities, your options are many, often free or low cost. Surprise yourself by trying something fun you've never done but think you might enjoy. We've taken a sushi class, tried rock climbing, watched a glass blowing exhibition and attended several cultural festivals.

3. Mix it up! Add variety. Just say no to fun ruts. Try something different every week.

4. Create a Fun Ideas Jar. Tear or cut a piece of paper into twenty squares. On each one, write a different suggestion for fun. If you need additional ideas, ask your family, friends or co-workers. Toss these in your jar and when you find your fun quota running low but are too exhausted to come up with an idea, reach into your idea jar and let the fun begin.

Chapter Four:
Stay Connected to the Source

Your sacred space is where you can find yourself again and again.

—*Joseph Campbell*

Dear You,

It's quite a process to remain connected to the Source of faith. There's convention. There's dogma. There's heritage, tradition, expectation and "all the things we have been taught." It's an unfortunate truth that judgment swirls around faith communities, not because of the principles inherent in belief, but rather because of shared humanity.

Engaging deeply with that "still small voice" of Spirit quiets all the noise and stills the rushing waters of shared human drama. An intimate and compelling measure comes from asking, "How can Spirit behave through me in this circumstance?" In the complexity of modern congregating, in any faith and the diverse dynamics of denominations and factions within each system, there is this fundamental principle: Source is engaged both within you and through you. In faith, you affiliate your soul, willingly, with the animating principle of the universe. To articulate and participate in that which is authentically holy and not simply habit means to embrace the All-ness of Source. Creation. Flow. Acceptance. Love. Compassion. Even attributes like shadow, storm, resistance. Source provides a mirror of Spirit in the very progression of the seasons that you mark on your calendar pages. Notice, then connect to their truth.

Love,

Your Life

I realize we don't all see God the same way. I tend to look at God more as a mother figure—resilient, responsible, loving and tender. Spirituality, or whatever you choose to call it, is our personal connection to the Source. For me, that's God, pure and simple. As a preacher's kid, I was convinced they called us the Moore family because we attended church more often than anyone else I knew. We filled a pew twice on Sundays, once on Wednesday nights and seven nights straight during week-long revivals. With Dad in the pulpit, it's safe to say I connected to my Source early on.

When I first came out, I agonized over how to reconcile my deep Christian faith with the realization that I was gay. In my church and personal belief system, people married and settled down. I wanted that, too. There were two insurmountable challenges: Gay marriage wasn't legal anywhere and my particular denomination taught that all gay people were bound for hell—in a hand basket. One night, after working the late shift at a high-end restaurant in Clearwater, I visited the cow pasture out back to commune with God.

We'd been on a first name basis forever so I just started in. "God, I'm in a real quandary here and I don't know what to do. You know me. You know who I am. You created me and you don't make mistakes. I can't ever see myself married to a man." I waited and as I stood there gazing up into the heavens, here's what I heard. "You are my child. I love you and would never ask you to do something that would make you miserable." I believe it was God's way of saying, "We're good here. Can we move on to more important things?" Through my Source, I experienced unconditional love for the very first time.

God is still my Source. I know there is something much bigger going on than us just playing Earth down here. Haven't you experienced those times when you couldn't comprehend why life was happening the way it was—good or bad—and then much later, you looked back on those same circumstances with understanding, wonder and awe, realizing they were stepping stones to where you are today? Me, too.

For years I couldn't understand why I lingered in a loveless relationship but later realized I was in a holding pattern, waiting for Pam. If I had chosen social work over accounting, Pam and I wouldn't soon be celebrating our twenty-fourth anniversary. If we hadn't gone to the West Coast for our first ever month-long vacation, I might never have heard of Mary Anne Radmacher and this book wouldn't be in your hands. These aren't coincidences; they are the miraculous synchronicities we discover throughout life. These are spiritual touches in our all-too-human lives, circumstances we could not have choreographed on our own if we had tried. They may go down in our personal histories as magic, but sacred is much closer to the truth.

> *Connecting to the Source opens our hearts to comfort, grace, gratitude, guidance and inspired relationships, infusing us with love for one another.*

Connecting to the Source opens our hearts to comfort, grace, gratitude, guidance and inspired relationships, infusing us with love for one another. Discover, rediscover or revel in the joy of connecting to your personal Source.

Try This:

1. Learn from your past willingness to walk in the world connected to your Source. Reflect on those times you received insight without asking. What has been your biggest learning? What evidence do you have to trust your Source even more deeply? Record this in your journal.
2. Offer up your concerns and your cares. List them or say them out loud. If you are comfortable, start with, "I'm turning this over to you... " Then turn them over, the same way you return a book to the library. You no longer own it. Let go. Take a deep breath. Let it out.
3. Seek guidance from your Source and listen for the response.
4. Find your Source community. Learn from others how to deepen your relationship with the Source that has your highest good in mind.

Bonus Try This:

Commit to deepening your understanding of the Source that nurtures and prepares you for your work in the larger world.

Check Your Gratitude Attitude

When we focus on our gratitude, the tide of disappointment goes out and the tide of love rushes in.

—*Kristin Armstrong*

Dear You,

In the face of challenge does it seem trite to begin a count of your blessings? Look at the swing of a pendulum for the answer. Everything is on a continuum. Each **THIS** is balanced on the other end of its line by a **THAT**. Challenge countered by blessing is not a shallow contradiction but a manifestation of the physics of a life.

So, sit down with another cuppa something and use a few of your rare, never-gonna-get-em-back minutes to count your blessings. Even if you have to start with the challenges in order to follow the line to the blessing. I see it all the time. What looks like an undesirable thing while it's happening turns out to be the turning point of somebody's life. Go ahead. One. Two. Three...

Love,

Your Life

Gratitude is the closest thing to magic that I've found. It's Aladdin's lamp on steroids. What else can instantly turn a gray day into one filled with sunshine? Gratitude lightens life by inspiring us to consciously search for nuggets of goodness and beauty.

During a family vacation, my brothers and I panned for gold, spending hours hunched over rusty pans sifting through red Georgia clay for the elusive sparkling flecks. Each discovery brought squeals of delight. We collected our finds in miniature water-filled bottles to take home as souvenirs—along with lessons for a lifetime.

Today we ask our coaching clients to sift through the details of their week in search of one nugget of gratitude to share during our session together. Recently, a new client couldn't think of anything to be grateful for. Not. One. Thing. She spent the entire hour focused on everything wrong in her life but couldn't spend 60 seconds on gratitude.

Much like determined treasure hunters, we eventually find what we seek. The person panning for gold will notice and delight in the smallest fleck, while those determined to see only dirt will find exactly that.

Your personal search for gold—the hidden beauty within each day—shapes your life. Gratitude isn't some Pollyannaish practice; gratitude allows us to absorb the richness in our lives regardless of the balance in our bank accounts. Choosing an attitude of gratitude profoundly upgrades your level of contentment. Simply put, the more grateful you are, the more grateful you become. Your gratitude is infectious. Expressing your gratitude to others is a precious act of love.

We extend gratitude to those in every area of our lives—for friends and family, for the medical team who cured me of cancer and the one who healed Pam's serious leg injury, for service people, safe drivers and the people who think up, build, service and pilot the airplanes we fly on. We often take for granted the miracles that fill our lives with ease. Spend an entire day thinking of every human who makes your life run smoothly. I can't get through that exercise without tears of gratitude streaming down my face and without thanking total strangers for the gifts they bring to this planet.

Make it a practice to liberally share your gratitude with everyone you interact with.

By habitually seeking out and noting the beauty, perfection or love in your days, gratitude deepens your connection to all of life and tunes your perception antenna to good. Even on life's most challenging days, you find

> *Gratitude centers you in the beauty known as now.*

what you seek. When you express your gratitude to others, waves of love ripple out.

Gratitude centers you in the beauty known as now.

Try This:

1. Set your daily gratitude intention and make a date with yourself to stop and hold space for gratitude. Your gratitude practice can be morning, evening or any time of day. Make it most convenient for you. Use this time to reflect on the blessings in your life.

2. Think of three things, people or situations you are profoundly grateful for right now. Reflect on whatever you've chosen for at least two full minutes. Notice what comes up for you. List your appreciations in your journal.

3. Share your gratitude with others, verbally and in writing. Begin by telling others the gratitude you have for them. It can be the person working the drive-through, someone in your home, or your office. I've stopped strangers on the street and thanked them for a loving act I witnessed. Express your gratitude in writing. Send a brief email or handwritten note of gratitude to someone who makes a difference in your life. I've sent them to co-workers, former teachers, our waste management people, clients and friends.

4. Begin your own gratitude journal. Capture your gratitudes for the day in writing. There are no rules except to write what moves you on that particular day. Some days, your gratitude may be as simple as getting out of bed. Every gratitude carries significance. Something or someone lightened your heart, opened your eyes to the beauty and love in the world. A gratitude journal is your private record of that journey.

Bonus Try This:

Invite a friend, partner or spouse to begin a brief gratitude practice with you. This can be in person, through social media or some other way. Each day, share your three gratitudes and listen as they share theirs. This practice is a natural intimacy builder as you begin to see the world through their eyes as well as your own.

Find Your Community

Community is first of all a quality of the heart. It grows from
the spiritual knowledge that we are alive not for ourselves
but for one another. Community is the fruit of our capacity to
make the interests of others more important than our own. The
question, therefore, is not 'How can we make community?'
but, 'How can we develop and nurture giving hearts?'

—*Henri Nouwen*

Dear You,

You have a community. Maybe more than one. They
might not even know each other, but they know
you. Such a group exists by virtue of a commonality.
Sometimes more than one commonality. The power of
a gathered people is strong. Be grateful and aware of
your circles of commonality. They feel close and yet
could dwell half the world away. In spite of distance,
they look a lot like a community. And act like one,
too.

How do you recognize a member of your community?
Two sure signs are when they are happy for your
success and hold space for you in a certain difficulty.

There are other signs as well—you'll know them when
you see them.

Love,

Your Life

As a writer, I wandered alone through the proverbial desert of dangling participles and run-on sentences for years before joining a small writing group made up of academics. I soon learned our writing styles could not have been more different as I found myself tidying up words, stripping my stories of life and color, dancing to their suggested edits while losing my writing voice. It was several years before I found my writing family, other creatives who spoke my language, sometimes without speaking at all.

At the urging of my writing mentor, Mary Anne (yes, that Mary Anne), I attended Patti Digh's first creativity camp and met a group of like-minded creatives from across the country and beyond. We came with name tags. That's it. No roster and no societal measuring stick for one another. We spent the weekend among highly successful authors, artists and other creatives, those just starting out and still others somewhere in between. The great thing was no one knew—or cared! Within moments I knew these were my people, or at the very least the neighbors of my soul. This was and is the essence of community—almost instantaneous acceptance, connection and caring at a heart level.

Throughout the weekend, in groups small and large, we learned each other's secrets, pulled for one another and shared our deepest longings. We heard spoken word poets who shattered our collective worlds as we each held our breath one moment and sobbed the next. We connected over activities and intimate conversations, stretching ourselves through the discomfort of the unknown. We laid ourselves bare against the fabric of togetherness. And when it was over, we wept because it was too soon—already missing the cocoon of camp.

Fortunately, camp ended only in the physical sense; we've since become neighbors of heart. Though scattered geographically, we regularly connect through social media—celebrating, encouraging, comforting and acknowledging one another's challenges and joys. Our group is part advice column, part cheerleading squad, part recipe exchange, part support system, part business incubator, and part prayer chain. Camp T-shirts have become a symbol of support for one another on the toughest of days. We're deeply attuned to the nuances of life within our community. Dare I say that we love one another? I'm certain of it.

> *When you hear your soul whisper,* These are my people, *pay attention.*

Although I've belonged to church groups for most of my life, this is the first sense of deep belonging I've found within the broader community. Perhaps because we are tied by heart and purpose, in some fashion, we all belong.

Keep looking. When you hear your soul whisper, *These are my people*, pay attention, settle in and actively participate.

Try This:

1. How do you know when a group of people resonates with you? When you have found a sense of heart-neighbors in the past, how did you know? Journal about your experience. What stood out for you?

2. Stay open to finding your community. Odds are, if you are receptive to finding them, eventually you will. Allow yourself to participate in new experiences; say yes to possibilities. Even though I was beyond nervous, I met my creative family by saying yes to camp.

3. Pay attention to those rare connections when you feel your heart whisper, *These are my people*. How will you follow up? How will you stay connected? Record your commitments in your journal.

4. Invest in your group. Bring your authentic self and your gifts to the table. Beyond an underlying connection, communities thrive when members participate reciprocally. Inside the circle, there is a magical exchange of energy. Offer up what you can and ask for assistance when needed. Membership is like dancing. While participation isn't mandatory, you'll get far more out of the experience if you are out on the floor rather than observing from the sidelines.

Trust Your Gut—Listen for Inspired Nudges

Signs don't shout; they whisper.

—A.D. Posey

Dear You,

You wonder a lot about dreams. There are different theories and you can't help but question if your dreams are the way your inner self tries to get your attention. The theory behind a dream, an impulse or an inspiration doesn't really matter, does it? I have lots of ways to get your attention and I'm not saying it's me and I'm not saying it isn't... The real point is that a dream is able to get your attention.

Once an inspired nudge gets your attention, I've noticed your habit of arguing with it. Immediately. You can almost be dismissive at times. Instead of looking at the nudge and letting it sink in, you launch right in to try to override the suggestion. In short, stop that. A nudge has to go to a lot of work to get you to pause long enough to even know it is there. So once you do see it, be a little more considerate in the time you spend considering. If you please. Thank you.

Love,

Your Life

Inspiration arrives at the most unexpected times. Pam and I visited Sanibel Island for a week of rejuvenation with my Mom. Since we've regularly vacationed there together, we have our own comfortable routines. Pam and I rise early to cycle and Mom heads out, usually before we awaken, to walk to the lighthouse and back, a distance of about five miles round trip. This particular visit, her knee was bothering her so she'd shortened her usual morning trek.

The last morning there for this visit, we woke up, dressed quickly, downed breakfast and headed out for our usual ride, But at the last minute, we decided to ride in the opposite direction. Cycling past pastel-colored homes with perfect lawns and yards filled with crushed shells in place of grass, we crossed several small bridges where canals crisscross the island. Finally, we arrived at the lighthouse parking lot.

On impulse, we decided to park the bike and take the boardwalk down to the beach. When the beach came into view, there was a familiar sight: Mom meandering down the beach collecting shells as she went. Pam called out her name and we quickly joined her at the water's edge. As we looked back in the direction of the condo, thick dark clouds clearly indicated a rapidly approaching storm.

Pam suggested we quickly ride back to the condo, grab the car and pick up Mom before the storm hit. Mom agreed to meet us at the shelter next to the road. We cycled fast, not wanting to get caught in the storm and wanting to make sure Mom was safe. While I stowed the bike, Pam grabbed the car keys and we headed back out. Mom was waiting for us, just where she said she would be. When she climbed into the car she said, "You know, the closer I got to the lighthouse, the more I hoped you two would be waiting for me so I wouldn't have to walk all the way back, but I know you never come this way. Still, I hoped it would happen."

We all grinned. What were the odds we would end up in the same place at the same time? Unlikely without love-inspired nudges and the willingness to hear and act on them.

When love-inspired nudges come, ACT!

Try This:

1. Ponder your experience with inspired nudges in the past. What do you call that still voice you hear within? If it doesn't have a name, does that matter? Record what comes up for you here.

2. Invite inspired nudges into your life. Get quiet and pay attention. Be open-hearted to what you hear or see. As long as you open the channel, your Source alerts you to opportunities to serve.

3. Honor your nudges. The next time you hear an inspired nudge, go with it. Take the long way home. Call your friend. Turn around and ask the person if they need assistance. Tuck a check or an inspirational quote into someone's card. Journal about your experiences in honoring your inspired nudges.

4. Welcome the nudges that invite self-care and compassion. Act kindly and quickly on those, too. What do they sound like and what is your response to them? Give them as much credence as you give inspired nudges for others. Journal about your experience in responding to self-care inspired nudges versus those for others.

Chapter Five:
Look for Opportunities to
Grow Your Capacity for Love

When we are willing to love beyond our comfort zone, we open the door to genuine relationship transformation.

—Marci Moore

Dear You,

Be mindful of the stories you carry. The stories that, unbidden, begin with, "Oh, not again—this always happens." Change that first line and you can change the whole story.

When you encounter an uncomfortably familiar story, invite yourself to rewrite the first sentence. And in conversation with another, in the absence of being able to say, "I understand you," it can be enough (and is sometimes ideal) to simply acknowledge, "I hear you." When you recognize the part you play in the "this always happens" scenario, you can consciously change your role. That willingness to trade in your familiar portion is the beginning of growing your capacity for love.

Love,

Your Life

Relationships aren't static but the stories we tell ourselves about them often are. Commit to seeing those you love through fresh eyes.

Twenty-one years ago, we came close to writing off part of my family. We'd just finished our commitment ceremony—the closest option to a wedding that existed at the time. Two of my brothers attended; one served as our best man. No one else in our families participated. When one brother returned to my parent's house that night still dressed in his tuxedo, another brother and my parents glanced up. None of them bothered asking him how the event went—then or ever. After that, he returned home and didn't speak to them for some time.

I'm embarrassed to say that I lasted for two months—long enough to miss the birth of my third nephew. I don't hold grudges. It's not in my nature. I'm known for leaving the door to relationship restoration open for years. But my heart ached and I needed time away to process what this meant for our ongoing relationship with my larger family.

During those two months I agonized over what to do and cried—a lot. Family is one of my top values. Pam and I spent numerous hours discussing our options. Finally, I came to her and said, "I can't walk away from my nephews. I want us to be the aunts that love unconditionally, like my Aunt Sylvia did. I have no idea how this will turn out. We could get the boot at any moment but until that day comes, I want to love on those boys. Are you in?"

> Commit to seeing those you love through fresh eyes.

Courageously, Pam said, "Yes." And love we did—and still do.

We helped babysit them at Mom and Dad's every Saturday night unless we were out of town—for thirteen years. When the nephews started private Christian school, we attended almost every sporting event, concert, art show and musical possible. We never pushed to be included; we simply showed up when and where we could, loving those little guys with all our hearts.

Relationship restoration happened tentatively and slowly. Impromptu family dinners sprung up around the nephews' events.

We began spending time with one another outside of school events. Our closeness grew, as relationships do, with time and attention. We sought and found common ground: Family means the world to all of us.

Together we've witnessed graduations and marriages and watched our family of origin shrink by two. Losses test the best of relationships and we are blessed to have come through them stronger and more unified than before. I believe love is responsible. Along the way we've all stretched. Instead of closing our hearts to one another, we've navigated the challenging terrain to continue building on the foundation of love we share. And we are better for it.

> *Instead of closing our hearts to one another, we've navigated the challenging terrain to continue building on the foundation of love we share. And we are better for it.*

From the outside, our differences still appear substantial enough to keep us oceans apart—yet we've found common ground. We choose to remain invested in one another's lives. We choose to celebrate what we can with and for one another. We choose not to ask one another for more than the other can give. We even take an annual siblings cruise together. Our relationship reminds me of what is possible for the rest of the world, when we dare supersize our definition of love.

The next time you are tempted to close your heart, consider supersizing your love instead.

Try This:

1. Find ways to appreciate what is and what you CAN do. We could see the boys at my parent's house every Saturday night. As they entered school, we could attend their sporting events. We got to cheer them on and watch each of them learn to read. We cherished every minute of watching them grow up and love the men they are becoming. What are ways you can stay in a relationship?

2. Lower your expectations. Look for the minimum that you'll accept. That might sound odd but if we'd held out for the whole enchilada, a grand welcome back into the family plus commitment ceremony cards and gifts or family asking to look at pictures of our ceremony, we'd probably still be waiting. What was important to us was being a part of the boys' lives. Everything else was pure bonus. What is the minimum you'll accept to stay in a relationship? Only you can decide what the minimum is.

3. Let love, not your differences, define your relationships. What is your common ground? At our very core, we were family and ALL of us loved those little boys. It was our starting place. What's yours?

4. Notice opportunities to open your heart. Our first impulse is to protect our hearts, to avoid putting ourselves in the position of being hurt. And there are certainly times when that makes sense. You don't want to put yourself in harm's way. When, where and how can you supersize your love?

Bonus Try This:

Consider opening your heart in a way you've resisted before. It would have been so easy to slam the door. We've learned to love in the crevices, in the places we are able and watch some of that love unfold into more robust relationships. That's happened in both of our families over time.

Allow Yourself to be Influenced

Blessed is the influence of one true, loving human soul on another.

—*George Eliot*

Dear You,

Know that coincidences can randomly occur and also know that sometimes they are more than coincidence. Viewing serendipitous events as a synergistic alignment of influence can be like seeing through cosmic windows. Understanding universal influences and allowing yourself to participate in them is not random but rather an important part of an intentional life. Really, almost a matter of faith.

Rather than leaning in to comfortable certainty, you can choose, instead, to embrace curiosity. A lot of people suggest that certainty is the opposite of uncertainty. Just between you and me, the opposite of certainty is curiosity. Curiosity has the courage to learn, to explore, to be content with not knowing. It is from this vulnerable and powerful place that you find the focus to allow yourself to be influenced by serendipity, by the Great Mystery. It's also a good time for learning. What a fine influence learning is.

While unsavory characters can exert influence on you (and I've noticed that from time to time they have), you can guarantee the quality of your influencers by choosing carefully the circle of peers and possibilities that you hang out and associate with. Wise folk have been observing for centuries that if you would really know a person—just take a close look at their closest circle of friends.

Love,

Your Life

I don't know everything. Chances are neither do you. Most of my significant personal growth came from welcoming positive influences into my life. Perhaps yours as well.

As children, we had little input into the people who influenced us. As adults, we can handpick them.

Carefully choose those you allow to influence you. Take the golden nuggets. Tuck them away or weave them into your own life. While this doesn't mean you copy another person, it does mean incorporating those beliefs, values and actions which resonate most deeply with you. Often, we're naturally surrounded with positive influences; other times, we must seek them out.

As my youngest brother rose through the ranks in medical sales, he carefully observed others who were highly successful. He paid attention to sales professionals and surgeons adept at developing strong professional relationships. Although quite young, he purposefully sought out as role models those individuals with balanced personal and professional lives. He chose men of integrity and faith to seek counsel from. Over time, these men influenced his employment decisions, the way he raised his children, his commitment to giving, his goals and ultimately the man he has become.

When Pam and I first began our life together, we each came with lifelong habits. I brought my family's two strongest communication tools: silence and a broom for sweeping uncomfortable conversations under the rug. Pam brought her family's unique communication style: no escape until an issue is resolved. Neither style worked particularly well in combination with the other. Fortunately, our love for one another far outweighed holding onto rusty, unworkable tools. We opened ourselves to one another's influence. Through trial, error and an ever-deepening trust for one another, we navigated the differences.

Since I'm naturally a processor and Pam a talker, I typically need space for reflection in the middle of difficult conversations. Often that meant Pam's need for closure took a back seat to my need for a time-out. If I requested a break, Pam generously gave me the space I needed. What she asked in return was my word on resuming the conversation once I was ready to talk. I promised and came back to the table. We met in the middle, trusting one another enough to experiment with an entirely new way of communication. It worked. As our new communication skills took root, we grew even closer.

Pam's influence impacted the trajectory of our consulting work as well. She models open communication and conflict resolution skills, something I'd learned bits and pieces of on the fly. Our early communication successes deeply informed our desire to teach others. We've since taken extensive training and taught thousands about communicating with love—even during conflict.

> **"** *Accepting positive influence is the ultimate "pass it on" of love.*

Accepting positive influence is the ultimate "pass it on" of love. By consciously learning from those who exemplify lives of integrity and love, and who positively influence the lives of others, you'll discover your own voice and approach to loving larger in the world.

Try This:

1. Think of the single greatest positive influence in your life. What impact did the person have on who you are today? Did you choose them immediately or did you accept their influence over time? Journal about your experience.

2. On a scale of one to ten, how purposeful are you about the people you allow to influence you? How does this show up in your life?

3. What criteria do you have for those you allow to influence you? How has this evolved over the years? Journal about what you've learned.

4. Think of someone you strongly admire. What is it that you admire about them? If the belief, value or action is not already a part of your life, how might you go about incorporating it? Eleanor Roosevelt is a much admired figure to Mary Anne. She often asks herself when she needs positive influence or guidance, "What Would Eleanor Do?"

Presume Loving Intent

Make it a practice to judge persons and things in the most
favorable light at all times and under all circumstances.

—Saint Vincent de Paul

Dear You,

The process of growing up takes everyone through
stages of self-knowing. You spend your life getting
to know yourself more thoroughly. Sometimes
people call it "carrying baggage,"—the process of
remembering things that have happened to you.
When it is framed by lessons that have been learned,
I call it experience, and I'm your life, so I would
know!

It takes a great deal of self-love and confidence
to presume loving intent. I know Hanlon's Razor
suggests you should first presume stupidity before
assuming malicious intent. That's pretty harsh.
(Although I take his point.) How about when you
observe someone's behavior, especially when it has
a negative impact on you, you opt to not take it
personally in the first place? Secondly, you choose to
presume loving intent instead of purposeful malice.
Maybe they'll call it Life's Razor some day! I believe
your system of justice requires a person be considered
innocent until proven guilty. This is kind of like
that. Until you have demonstration of some other
truth, I suggest you start with love.

In general, while I'm talking about intent, I think
those three words are the best recipe for personal
success I could offer: Start With Love.

Love,

Your Life

71

At the beginning of an exciting candidate search to fill the chief development officer position for a local nonprofit, I reconnected with a promising candidate from an earlier search. After listening intently to my description of the opportunity, she expressed great interest. Before hanging up we made plans to talk within the week. Then she fell off the radar screen—not returning a single call or email.

Perplexed, I thought back to what I knew of her. All our previous conversations indicated she was the consummate professional. I told Pam, "I just don't understand. Something must have come up." I continued reviewing resumes and contacting other candidates. Still, whenever I saw her name on the candidate roster, I wondered what had happened. Ten days later she called, deeply apologetic for not responding more quickly, and hurriedly explained.

Within hours of our initial call, she'd had emergency surgery and was just getting back on her feet. I was able to honestly say, "I knew something must have come up."

I could have easily misinterpreted my candidate's disappearance as thoughtless and rude. I could have assumed she accepted another offer. As humans, we love to fill in the blanks by creating elaborate stories. By the time she called I might have been guarded in my response instead of warm and inviting. A negative story could have permanently impacted our relationship.

Before email and social media, a dear friend who lived out of state stopped communicating. I missed her and didn't understand what happened, but kept sending letters as if nothing had—for three years. When she finally wrote, she apologized and said she understood if I didn't want to be friends any longer. Her three-page letter filled in the blanks. She'd divorced her husband. Working full time and raising two young children as a single mom took everything she had. When she resurfaced, she reached out. I reached back. There were no hard feelings. I loved her through whatever was happening in her life. I loved her with no expectations. We've been friends since we were nineteen years old with a blip somewhere in the middle. We are closer today than we've ever been. Had I made up stories and hardened my heart, we wouldn't be celebrating the robust friendship we share today.

When you refuse to assign stories or emotions to other people's behavior, you preserve the possibility of an ongoing relationship. By presuming loving intent, you remain open and curious.

Try This:

1. Practice presuming loving intent while driving your car this week. When you notice another driver speeding, imagine the potential loving intent behind their actions. I often picture speeders racing to visit a loved one in the hospital or to pick up an ill child from school. If someone takes your perfect parking spot, try thinking, "Wow, they must need to be closer to the store entrance than I do." Notice how these simple words instantly transform your feelings toward the other person.
2. Notice each time you find yourself making up a story about another person's intention. **Note**: Anything other than absolute fact is, by definition, a story. Ask yourself, what loving intent might that person have right now? Try to think of five alternative positive stories that might be true. Allow yourself to wonder. If you naturally fill in the blanks, let it be with love.
3. Make a deeper commitment to retrain your brain to presume loving intent. Invite curiosity into your life. When you notice yourself making up a story about a situation, stop. Practice sitting with the unknown without making the other person wrong.
4. Reflect on whether you have damaged any relationships based on stories you created to explain another person's actions. If so, journal about your experience. What did you discover? Once you have clarity, if you are so inclined, reach out. One place to start is with heartfelt apology.

Dive in Head First

Sometimes grace works like water wings
when you feel like you are sinking.

—*Anne Lamott*

Dear You,

There are logical reasons and honest objections against the advice to "dive in head first." Common sense is often confused with genuine apprehension (which sounds like, "What if it doesn't work?" "What if they don't like what I offer?"). It can be time consuming to sort through the difference between an informed gut instinct and anxiety; they share some similarities. It's worth the time. Trust me on this.

The inclination to dive in, fully engaged, is tempered by a desire to avoid hurt or embarrassment. It's tempting to institute "trial periods" when you get to be halfway in and "just see" what it's like. Here's the thing—you can't fully see a thing when you are only halfway in. Your view is impaired. And you can't halfway dive off the diving board.

A wholehearted commitment is essential to be all in with something or someone. When experience and instinct intersect with information, you're in a sweet spot of confidence and even ease. Only you know, only you have the instinct as to whether a particular fully committed dive off the high diving board is right for you.

Love,

Your Life

Life changes in an instant. Still reeling from my older brother Mark's death 26 days earlier, Pam and I were heading out for a much-needed getaway when my brother Joel called.

"Sis, where are you?"

"We're leaving the house now. We got a late start."

He interrupted me. "Dad's at the ER. He's unresponsive. Mom and Amy are already there. Marvin is on his way."

When I dropped the luggage to put a hand over my mouth, Pam knew it was the call we'd been dreading. She released her bag, took my hand and together we raced for the car. Joel told me what little he knew as Pam and I raced toward the hospital.

In the emergency room and the hours that followed, we waited for Dad's doctors to give us a single sliver of hope, but received none. We learned to lean into and through our individual fears as much for each other as for Mom. We took turns making the difficult phone calls to family and friends.

Together we spent the next two days as a single unit making medical decisions no one wants to make. As the doctor gently unhooked Dad from the machines keeping his body alive, we sobbed, clinging to one another like survivors in a lifeboat tipping dangerously to one side. The man we knew as Dad was gone even though his heart kept beating.

A nurse silenced the cacophony of beeps in Dad's room. We turned on soft Christian music and, standing around his bed, shared story after story of life with Dad, alternating between laughter and sobs. We held Dad's beefy hands, now still and rubbed his arms. Friends came to say their goodbyes.

We finally sent Mom home to rest. Amy and Pam headed out on separate errands. I was alone, scared Dad would leave us on my watch. And he did, but not until we shared a few minutes alone. I thanked him for his constant love and support, prayed aloud, repeated one of his favorite knock-knock jokes and said goodbye. I held his hand and kissed the top of his head, surprised by the prickly stubble of growth.

An alarm split the silence between us. In confusion, I looked around the room for the source of the noise. Dad's heart had stopped. I stood over him, one hand on his arm, another on his shoulder, faces almost touching and begged, "Dad, Mom will be here in five minutes. Please don't go." In response, the flat green line lifted, creating irregular peaks for a solid minute before forever flattening.

> *I learned that loving deeply means going through, not around, life's inevitable storms.*

Not only was I able to be with Dad in his final moments, but I was able to tell Mom that he was gone. To this day I have no idea what I said. Love gave me the words. Without what came before—without my experience caring for Mark, I might have bolted. Instead, I learned that loving deeply means going through, not around, life's inevitable storms. Since that day, I'm more at ease comforting others, trusting that love will always give me the words.

Our greatest growth as human beings takes place during the deepest dives into the unknown—for love's sake.

Remember, you are never given an assignment to fly without the ability to carry it out, even if it means growing your wings along the way.

Try This:

1. Practice saying yes to the unexpected. This gives you the courage and confidence to say yes to larger requests. Write about your experiences.
2. Think of a time when you've taken the plunge and surprised yourself by doing something you had no idea you could do. What did you carry away from that experience?
3. Commit to show up when you are called on. Trust that Spirit or The Universe will provide you the strength and internal fortitude to navigate whatever lies ahead.
4. Let love be your guide. Love is far larger than our fears. Ask yourself, what would love do, and then do it. Love would visit a friend in the hospital. Love would attend a funeral to support a close friend. Love would sit quietly with a friend who recently received a difficult diagnosis. Expect to be uncomfortable at first but dive in anyway. No one teaches us how to navigate difficult journeys. These learnings come through the experiences themselves—you bravely standing in the moment and loving with all of your being. Journal about your sacred experiences, when you're uncertain of your preparedness but use love as your guide. Mine for the nuggets you've unearthed.

Chapter Six: Be Present

If you surrender completely to moments as they
pass, you live more richly those moments.

—*Anne Morrow Lindbergh*

Dear You,

How kind you are to animals says a lot about you.
The precision with which you make considered
decisions is also something I appreciate. You have
a unique awareness of the time of day and how
dramatically different the light is at dawn than at
dusk. You have a real willingness to explore what
others suggest, even when it brushes up against a
differing view you hold. I can tell you are giving
someone the respect of being influenced by them
when you allow, "Well, may-be..."

Your capacity to see extends beyond geography,
beyond physics, beyond time. Just ask any of your
friends who ask you, "How did you know to call
right now?" You are unfailingly kind even when you
are delivering a "no" to someone you care about. You
are equally kind, and enthusiastic, when you offer a
YES. Of course I notice. I am present to you, at least
all the times that you allow me to be! I notice you
seem to be on a perennial search for balance. I want
to give you an assurance for the times when it seems
balance does not show up for you. It is elusive in
the small and the calendared. Balance dwells in the
aggregate and the overall. In looking back on your
life it will be revealed that you were wholly (and
holy) attentive to each present moment. You could get
a head start on that future knowing and appreciate
that you are fully present now. Go ahead. Know it.

Love,

Your Life

When Mom was diagnosed with breast cancer twenty-four years ago, it was my first real brush with the uncertainty of life. As the social worker talked with Dad and me in the waiting room, I listened intently, realizing our world forever changed in that moment. Certain became uncertain. Promises became maybes. Life became immeasurably more precious.

After Mom came out of recovery, we talked for a bit. I remember walking to the car in a daze, climbing inside and laying my forehead on the steering wheel. What kept echoing in my heart was, life is not a dress rehearsal. Today is all we get. Tomorrow is a possibility, not a guarantee. It wasn't morbid; it was an eye-opener. It was more than enough to rouse me from sleepwalking through life, hoping people knew how much I loved and appreciated them. Mom's cancer diagnosis fueled me to consciously be present with others, to love all out and to let others know, regularly, how much I love them.

I started drinking people in. Instead of simply clinging to the periphery of gatherings, I began seeking out the beauty within each person, seeing them for their unique contributions to the planet. Today, I connect with others on a soul level. I want to know you, not just the face you present to the world.

People aren't interruptions in your day; they are the reason you are here.

When you choose to be fully present, daily life becomes richer as your interactions with others become more intimate. People aren't interruptions in your day; they are the reason you are here.

Your ability to be present with others is the original gift that keeps on giving. Conversations take on a new level of importance. People know you won't rush them and that when you say, "Being here with you is the most important use of my time in this moment," you mean it. They can relax. People feel held, deeply loved and appreciated in your presence.

Being present shows up in myriad ways—listening, encouraging, acknowledging, accepting and just being with others. Sometimes your presence, even without speaking, is the greatest gift of all.

During seven months of chemo, friends from all over the country took turns caring for me while Pam worked. They took me to doctor appointments, fixed special foods, made sure I drank enough fluids between naps, picked up our mail, ran errands and when I was awake, conversed with me. I couldn't have asked for a more attentive presence parade.

And isn't that what others want from us—our attention? To know that we are all-in when we spend time together?

I am definitely all in. How about you?

Try This:

1. Think back to a time when you have been fully present for another person. Journal about your experience. When did you become aware you were fully present? How did you come to that realization? How were you able to stay present throughout the experience?

2. Prepare yourself to be fully present with others. Clear your mind of worries or to-dos. Make a list. Yes, even list your worries so you won't lose track of them. Think of the person you will be spending time with. Hold their best interests at heart. Do some deep breathing. If you have concerns, discuss them ahead of time with a trusted friend. Ask Spirit or the Universe for the ability to be fully present and the words necessary to be supportive. If possible, block out time to be present. I find I am able to be fully present when I can relax into the time together without concern for rushing off to another appointment.

3. Minimize obstacles that could prevent you from giving another your full attention. Eliminate as many distractions as possible. Turn off the tech including your phone. In an office setting or at home, turn away from your computer and face the person. If you wear a watch, put it in your purse or pocket. Sit closer. Remove physical barriers. What do you notice about the quality of your conversation when you "make room" for being present?

4. Make eye contact. Listen attentively. Do your absolute best to come from a place of genuine curiosity. Nothing halts a conversation faster than judgment—whether through the words you use or in your facial expressions. Let conversations unfold rather than rushing through. Be yourself. If you are comfortable, ask what the person needs the most right now. They will let you know. What changes are you noticing in yourself and others as you build your "presence" muscle?

Shift Your Focus

If you don't like something change it; if you can't
change it, change the way you think about it.

—*Mary Engelbreit*

Dear You,

I've been telling you in so many ways that your
most important textbook is out your door. The rocks
under your feet have seen stories that you can barely
imagine (but do try!). That tree? That one bent
sideways in the wind? That you pass without notice?
Yeah, I put that there to teach you about resilience.
The detour that annoyed you just last week? I was
trying to get you to notice a new route but your
annoyance used up all your focus. I know it's sneaky
on my part, yet often those diversions are the only
way I have to capture your attention. Sometimes it
works. The inconveniences that change your plans
aren't always my doing, but sometimes they are. I
like to keep you guessing.

Love,

Your Life

Mary Anne recalls the time she needed directions:

The helpful desk clerk reeled off a series of "go this way and then turn on this road until the petrol station and when you come to a T, turn left. Right soon the property will be on your right."

Was it jet leg? Was it the quick speed with which she spoke or the familiarity she had with the area in which she had grown up? For whatever reason, I did take a route that was *comparable* to her directions but not *precisely* what she had told me to do.

I was looking for the property on the right. My perspective informed me that I was looking for a building and it would be on the right. Many kilometers and an hour later, another call was made. "Stay put. You're so close. I'll come for you"

In a few minutes, a car pulled up and a friendly wave let me know the driver of this vehicle was my pathfinder. Just two blocks away on the left was a *sign* for my desired destination. I'd been looking for the actual property as well as looking on the other side of the road. It never occurred to me to look on both sides for my destination or a sign.

Had I followed the directions with precision, it might've gone differently. If I had shifted my focus from a micro view to a macro, I would have allowed for looking on both sides of the road, or looking for something other than the building itself. I was so keyed into what I thought I knew that I spent an hour being lost. It so happens I'd driven past the sign twice and missed it completely because I was so focused on looking for a building, not a sign.

Try This:

1. Go a different way. Be willing to get lost for the sake of discovery.
2. Ask questions, especially of people you do not know well. Ask "How do you see this?" Consider asking more questions if they are willing to answer. New information may change the way you are looking at a thing.
3. Ask yourself, "What else might this be or mean?" Just like looking at a piece of cut crystal, looking through a different facet gives you a different perspective.
4. Mary Ann Evans as George Eliot wrote, "It's a narrow mind which cannot look at a subject from various points of view." Professor Wallace Roark, author of *Think Like an Octopus*, calls that "on the other hand thinking." Practice it often.

Say Goodbye to Otherizing

It is not our purpose to become each other; it is to recognize each other, to learn to see the other and honor him for what he is.

—Hermann Hesse

Dear You,

Do not let an unknown other be invisible to you. Seeing someone does not require verbal or physical engagement, seeing is engagement enough. Acknowledgement does not require additional action, it is action enough. Begin the work of acceptance simply by observing, noticing. "I see you," is a step toward a stronger and more unified world.

Bearing Witness. It's used in your legal system. In marriage ceremonies the bride and groom have to have witnesses sign their license. Being seen and seeing are such significant acts that they are woven into systems of law and culture.

I can't help but smile at the countless times I get to see new parents asking the brand new baby, "Where's Baby?" (I won't spoil it for you but I'm gonna suggest the baby knows they aren't the ones missing.) "There you are. We see you," the new parents coo. In spite of baby being slightly concerned that they've landed themselves with maybe not the brightest parents—Can't they see I've been here all along?—baby is still very pleased that the parents see and know where baby is!

We all need witness to our being. It makes us feel inclined, embraced and welcomed. It turns someone from a **them** into an **us**.

Love,

Your Life

Pam instantly knows that I'm frustrated with someone when I call them "that man" or "that woman" instead of referring to them by name when the two of us are talking. She noticed and pointed it out to me several years ago. It doesn't happen often but it's become a verbal red flag of awareness for me because in that moment, I am temporarily distancing myself from that individual with language. It's one example of what is called otherizing or making a distinction between another person and ourselves for the purpose of feeling superior or diminishing them in some way. We otherize in many ways every day, drawing lines of distinction based on religion, race, beliefs, marital status, sexual orientation, gender, gender identity, citizenship or language. We can otherize based on just about any-thing at all including age, body shape or clothing, among other, truly trivial things.

We otherize whenever we point to another human or group of humans and stress the differences rather than celebrate the simi-larities. Even in our own families we may otherize—at least I'm not the alcoholic one or the gay one or the mean one. I belong, we may tell ourselves. They don't. In the larger world, we split ourselves into small, manageable groups, typically filled with people just like us. Yet this doesn't mean that other groups or the members of those groups are any less valuable or any less human.

It's easy to love our own—our families, our extended families, our friends and those who agree with us. The real challenge is in loving those we consider most unlike ourselves, those whose families don't mirror our own or those whose beliefs we don't understand. Otherizing comes from fear. Fear and love cannot co-exist. Choose love and watch your perspective instantly shift.

> *Fear and love cannot co-exist. Choose love and watch your perspective instantly shift.*

Republican Senator Rob Portman, elected from Ohio in 2011, vowed to fight any forward movement on gay rights—until his own son came out to him. At that point, fatherly love won out. Senator Portman eventually supported equal rights for everyone. Ask yourself. Must a family member suffer discrimination, inequality, bullying or indifference before it matters to you? Make the commitment to stop otherizing today.

We need more compassion and far less otherizing. We need more empathy and less judgment. We need more understanding and inclusion. We need to embrace our fellow human beings. As Hillary Clinton has been known to say, "We need more love and kindness in our country." Instead of otherizing, imagine yourself in someone else's shoes and ask, what would love do? How would love treat the person you are thinking of? Do that.

As an out lesbian, I've spent a lifetime on the dark side of otherizing, excluded from the church I grew up in, denied both employment and housing, ridiculed and called names. I've had to excel in almost every area of my life just to feel equal to others. I've been one of those sitting on the sidelines praying pick me, pick me just the way I am. Every. Human. Matters. Equally. No matter what. No one should have to earn their equality.

Try This:

1. Seek common ground. The next time you have the opportunity to get to know someone you see as different from yourself, spend a few moments discovering what you have in common.

2. Stay open to love. The next time you find yourself getting worked up over another group's rights or status, ask yourself, what might I want for this person or group if they were members of my immediate family? What steps can I take to help make that happen? How might I become an ally?

3. Connect with your compassionate self. Whenever you see a group of people, look at them individually and send love. As you look at each person, say to yourself, *I love you* or if that makes you uncomfortable, just say, *love*. Repeat it over and over as you look from one person to the next. It's impossible to otherize our fellow human beings when we see them as just like us, someone with parents and siblings, when we recognize they are important to someone. Journal about your experience.

4. If you find yourself in a group of people who begin otherizing, stand up for love. Say, that person or these people matter. Find your voice. If you find yourself beginning to say something negative about a group of people, stop. See them as your fellow human beings. Writer and pastor John Pavlovitz began asking Christians to examine their hearts when it comes to LGBTQ people. He received hundreds of hateful comments. Instead of allowing it to stop him, he turned his blog pulpit into open arms, welcoming gay, lesbian, bi and transgendered people of faith. He now spends his days educating the public about the similarities we share, reminding parents how much love they felt for their child when he or she was born and asking them to still see their child through the same lens of unconditional love. Lately he has taken to reminding Christians to stop otherizing different religions, immigrants and refugees. When is the last time you have stood up when friends or family are otherizing? If you haven't, when will you?

Seek training to eliminate your tendency to otherize and learn how to become an ally to any group you feel called to serve. Start here: http://www.guidetoallyship.com/. Search the word ally. Don't just read. Do the work.

No Love Is Too Small

No act of kindness, however small, is ever wasted.

— Aesop

Dear You,

Use what you have. It's tempting to defer some loving potential until the more ideal circumstance comes along: "Until I'm not so busy; I have more money; I have something really big to give them." You might have a different set of "untils." What if you acted on your impulse for a loving gesture action right now, using the resources that are already available to you? What if you did what you could, right now, right where you are? There is no love that is too small. You may be thinking you need a whole new vehicle when the keys to your loving journey are already in your pocket. Take a look. You have greater resources than you imagine.

And sometimes what love requires isn't a thing at all, it's you. Your genuine self showing up with what love you've got. It sounds redundant but it's a loop of truth: Love is love. And it's always enough.

Love,

Your Life

Friends regularly inspire me through their small but mighty acts of love. One sends gourmet chocolate bars to delighted recipients—just because. Some tuck positive quote cards into visible places for co-workers and strangers to discover. Some artists leave small creations tucked into nooks along city sidewalks or in trees for others to stumble upon and claim. Others hold online fundraisers for friends in need.

You can always be love, in this very moment, wherever you are. Noticing is the key. Pay attention to those you share the world with. Consciously seek out opportunities to love.

Shower those in and around your home with love. Tuck I love you notes where the special people in your life will discover them. Catch those in your home doing something right. Give high fives all around. Disconnect the tech and gift loved ones with ten minutes, a mealtime or an entire day focused on them, free of electronics.

Volunteer to grocery shop or watch your significant other's favorite movie—for the fifth time. Hug. Often. Just because. Attend your loved ones' special events. Your presence matters. Ask others, what would you most like to do? Then do that.

Put a vibrant message on your voicemail. Report delivery people for their outstanding service. On garbage day, perch a six pack of soda on your trash can with a giant thank you note attached. Deliver a cold sports drink to your lawn or maintenance person.

Love the people sharing the road with you. Give yourself plenty of time to get where you are going. Give other cars plenty of space. Graciously let other drivers in front of you. Smile and wave when someone cuts you off. By maintaining your calm, you are doing your part to keep the road safe. Save non-emergency communications for when you aren't driving.

Start your workday with enthusiasm. It's contagious. Bring healthy snacks to share at the office. Celebrate co-workers' successes. Celebrate your co-workers' birthdays. Pass a hat—literally. Pass a birthday hat that sits on the birthday person's desk all day long. Learn an entirely new version of the happy birthday song and sing it. Offer assistance. Acknowledge others. Offer condolences. Ask, what would be most helpful to you right now?

At the grocery store, offer to grab an item off the top shelf for a fellow shopper who can't quite reach it. Help a lost shopper find the item they are looking for. Call for a cleanup in aisle three. Invite someone with a limited number of items to move ahead of you in the checkout line. Compliment the cashier. Return your grocery cart. The baggers will love you. Offer to return someone else's cart and you'll make two people happy!

Participate in your community. Get to know your neighbors. Walk whenever possible. Talk with those you meet. Shop locally. Cheer on total strangers in a local marathon. Show up, shout encouragement, ring a cow bell or clap for every person who runs past.

Pick up litter. Participate in or contribute to fundraisers. Volunteer. Vote.

These are just starter ideas. Get creative. The more ideas you come up with, the more love you'll spread. You'll begin to see the impact your love has on those around you. You may even inspire others to start their own love campaign.

Try This:

1. How have you shown up with love in the past? What have you most enjoyed? Journal about this.
2. Look over the list above. Decide where you'd like to plug in to love larger in a small way.
3. Choose a small positive love addition for each area—home, neighborhood, community, workplace, place of worship or other areas that make sense for you. Spread the love.
4. Commit to one or two small ways of showing up with love regularly. Notice how it impacts you. Notice how it impacts others. Journal about your experience.

Chapter Seven:
Show Up Spontaneously

I hope you're proud of yourself for the times you've said "yes," when all it meant was extra work for you and was seemingly helpful only to somebody else.

—Fred Rogers

Dear You,

Schedule. Spontaneity. They seem contradictory, don't they?

Imagine these are the names of two very earnest competitors engaged in an arm wrestling match. On the table, between the two of them, is YOUR planning calendar. That thing that you ask so much from. Help me! Keep my promises! Assist me to show up on time. Reveal to me sylvan spaces where I might rest, pause, recreate. The calendar that vacillates between serving your needs and insisting that you bow to its wishes. How many times does a friend offer you some delectable experience and you have to say, "Let me check my calendar?" Like your calendar is the boss of you? Both in the calendar blocks that are fully written in and the segments that remain blank (still open to possibility) lies the opportunity to seize the spontaneous moment. Word. Gesture. Event. There are those perennial planners who, with cheerful, colorful markers block off moments in the course of their commitments to "be spontaneous." Yes. They "schedule spontaneity."

The greater opportunity for spontaneity comes in the capacity to pivot. To be so in flow with a moment that you see beyond immediate plans to a more profound purpose. Plans gone awry become, instead of disappointment, an inspiration for the unanticipated joy, the surprise compassionate act of service, the whimsical wander. When you consider the stories that you repeatedly share, you'll discover the common thread is the capacity to pivot (and enjoy) the spontaneous. When it arrives. Uninvited. Hear that? It's the door, I'll let you go so you can see what fun has come knocking.

Love,

Your Life

Don't you sometimes wish love came with a detailed set of instructions like those you receive with games, new appliances or build-it-yourself furniture kits? Don't you wish you knew precisely when to leap out there? Deliberate spontaneity is the willingness to be loving when and where you land: online, in your car, on a bus, train or plane, in line at a fast food restaurant, in a doctor's office waiting room, at the gym, in your workplace and yes, even on vacation.

My friend, Lisa Vetter, recently shared her own experience with spontaneity. Let me retell it here:

When a late-night flight was cancelled due to a fast-approaching winter storm and the plane returned to the gate, passengers hustled back into the terminal only to be told there were no hotel rooms available. Cranky, exhausted and at their wits' end, many hunkered down calling friends and family while others texted, read, played on their phones or found spaces on the floor to sleep.

One gentleman generously shared the electrical charging station, unplugging his own devices so that others could revive theirs. His spur-of-the-moment invitation opened the door for conversation and connection. As others joined in, the diverse group planned and executed a food and coffee run, voluntarily taking and delivering orders for other passengers. During the food run, they spontaneously ordered chicken nuggets for children in the waiting lounge.

Later, as others slept, they talked quietly together, sharing names and life experiences, transforming strangers thrown together by happenstance into friends sharing an adventure. By morning, they'd exchanged contact information and agreed to continue their conversation onto their rescheduled flight and beyond.

No one person orchestrated this. These spontaneous acts of love and generosity unfolded throughout the night along with shared laughter and deepening friendships. I'd like to think that our instructions for times like this come directly from the Divine.

When a rare snowstorm stranded thousands of motorists in Atlanta, citizens and those in outlying suburbs, graciously opened their homes, Southern-style hospitality flooded social media outlets with offers of food and housing to those stranded.

Others soon joined in, including fire stations, shelters, and a grocery store.

Spontaneity is the ultimate pass it on of love. Individual stories pass from person to person. These retellings serve as continuous seeds of inspiration for the recipient and every person hearing them.

> *Spontaneity happens when you fling yourself into the fullness of life with the willingness of a skydiver.*

Spontaneity happens when you fling yourself into the fullness of life with the willingness of a skydiver. Part of the adventure involves presence. The only way to spontaneously show up is to engage all of your senses. Take in the cacophony of noise, the movements of others, facial expressions, tone of voice and body language. Be a love detective. Who could use a bit of your love today?

Try This:

1. Reflect on times in the past when you've shown up spontaneously. What did you take away from your experiences? Journal about your discoveries. Recently Pam was shopping at a local natural foods store. In one aisle, a clerk was pushing a dolly piled high with boxes. Pam stepped aside, pressing her back against the grocery shelving to give him plenty of room to maneuver. A minute later, he approached her. "Ma'am. Thanks for doing that... for stepping out of the way. Most people don't even notice me." Even the smallest spontaneous acts matter. As Pam later reflected on the experience, she decided to be more purposefully mindful of those around her.

2. Build tiny cushions of time into your schedule for spontaneity. By building in time reserves, you can talk when someone asks if you have a few minutes. Leave five minutes earlier for appointments. That way, when you see a car stranded in the middle of the road, you can offer assistance instead of feeling annoyed and driving past. Once you've practiced building in mini time buffers, journal about your experience.

3. Notice opportunities to spontaneously love on your fellow human beings. Act on them. Let a co-worker know you are headed out for lunch. See if there is anything you can pick up for them. Offer up your discount card to another person standing in line. Leave an unusually generous tip for a server having a rough day. If someone ahead of you drops something, pick it up and hand it to them. When you read an article that makes you think of someone, send it to them and say, I thought you might enjoy this. If someone needs a hug, make the offer. The more comfortable you grow with showing up spontaneously in small ways, the more apt you are to leap in when larger opportunities arise.

4. Continually practice spontaneity. Practice keeping your heart open to where and when you might show up. When you find yourself saying or thinking, *Well, that isn't in the plan for today*, ask yourself, *How might I make the time?*

Willingness—Love Says Yes

The big question is whether you are going to be able to say a hearty yes to your adventure.

—*Joseph Campbell*

Dear You,

When you arrived on this swiftly-turning planet, I made sure you were greeted with a giant YES. I wanted you to know, as quickly as possible, what it was like to have love say yes to you. I like to model the behavior that I want you to be able to participate in more freely. The world delivers affirmative responses to you in so many ways. If you are blessed to have an abundant water source, you understand that fundamental yes. Flowers. Wildlife. The love of a friend. And the love of a creature. Oh, and trees. Ah. I get distracted with all the wonderful YESes that are available.

To my point... you started out delivered on the wings of a lovely YES. As you grow in your place on the planet, it becomes part of your opportunity to say YES back. Say YES to the planet. YES to unexpected opportunities to serve, learn, assist, soar, play. Saying YES to love may not fit easily into that list of things to do you are carrying around and yet it is easily accommodated in your heart. Go there—you'll find the room.

Love,

Your Life

At the state fair entrance, twelve-year-old Joshua declared, "Last year I rode all the kiddie rides; this year I want to ride the big ones."

Upon hearing his son's words, my brother Paul, infamous for spew-inducing motion sickness, glanced at me uneasily. Few rides at the fair meet his no spinning, no swooping rule.

Joshua kept at it, "Somebody will go on the roller coaster with me, right?"

None of us wanted to volunteer, but that's what aunts do, at least aunts without kids, aunts that want to live up to a certain coolness factor and be remembered for sacrificing (I mean having fun...).

"If no one else will ride, I will." I heard myself saying.

He pointed at the wooden roller coaster. "I want to go on that one."

It was easily the Goliath of coasters on the fairgrounds. My eyes involuntarily followed the tracks, which rose, fell and looped dangerously; my chest tightened as if someone had just said, "Wait until your father gets home."

"Let's look around a bit, then pick out the rides you want to go on," Paul said.

He and Josh ended up exploring two fun houses, smashing into one another on the bumper cars and zooming down a log flume ride. Josh and I played midway games until he claimed a suitable prize. We kept finding other things to do and eat, staying away from the coaster. As we used ticket after ticket, I repeatedly prayed Josh would forget. That particular prayer went unanswered.

"We still have to ride the coaster before we leave," he reminded. Reluctantly, I followed him towards the monstrosity, my heart pounding as if I'd just run a marathon. The line stretched more than a hundred people deep. This fact did not faze Joshua. Together he and I took our places in line, eventually climbing into our seats: the first one in the front car. Joshua was giddy—another wish granted. I was terrified.

We lowered the safety bar and stared at each other for a moment with one of those, "Can you believe we're really doing this?" looks, until the car jerked forward. As it began to climb the first steep hill, each metallic click ricocheting in my ears, we raised our arms skyward. If I was going to do this thing, then I was going to do it all out! Once we crested the top, the car plummeted downward, quickly arcing into the next climb. We alternated between laughter and screaming, more focused on clutching the safety bar than keeping our hands raised high. By the time we climbed out, shaken but still smiling, we'd bonded more deeply because love said yes.

Try This:

1. Just say yes. Short of leaping out of an airplane, there are few things I wouldn't say yes to when it comes to my niece or nephews unless they are illegal, immoral, and unethical or would jeopardize them in any way. Find ways to say yes in the moment.

2. Say yes to strangers. Give the dollar, give directions, give a hand and if you are comfortable, give a lift. I once gave a bicycling camper in a remote state park a lift to get firewood. When he approached our camp, he looked cold and miserable. I felt no fear, just compassion toward this young man looking for a way to warm up and dry off after a long day on his bike. Pam was sure I'd just driven from the campsite with an axe murderer. My heart told me differently. We helped one another that day. He stretched my ability to trust. I helped him rest more comfortably that night. How can you safely start stretching your yeses to encompass those you don't know?

3. Say yes to loved ones. My aunt wanted a swimming pool in the worst possible way. Not only did she love to swim but with her knees worsening with each passing month, it was the one place she could exercise pain-free. She knew they could easily afford one but my uncle was a tightwad to a fault. After so many "Noes" over the years, she was hesitant to broach the topic. My mom encouraged her. When my aunt finally asked, as difficult as it was for him, my uncle said yes. Within a month my aunt was doing the breaststroke in her own backyard. Is there something you might say yes to for someone you love?

4. Move beyond your comfort zone. Many of us live tightly defined lives, cocoons really. We limit the ways we can love others. Saying yes starts with making eye contact. Does that make us a mark for people looking for money to buy beer or cigarettes? Probably. But it also means I'm open to help others. Instead of automatically saying no, ask, "Can I think about it?" I'm a bit of a processor which means if I respond too quickly it might not be my final answer, not because I was lying before but because

I didn't take the time needed to think it through. If I spend a few extra minutes, I might still say yes but it will be a real yes. It will be my leap from the airplane. Say yes to something that will keep you up later than usual. Say yes to an experience you can have with a loved one or something you can give a loved one. Say yes to love.

Adapt the Map

It is not the strongest of the species that survive, nor the most intelligent, but the one most responsive to change.

—*Charles Darwin*

Dear You,

There are maps. Plans. Itineraries. Then... there's what actually happens! Every so often they are the same thing. Mostly? Not. It is easy to become vested in planning and mapping out. Almost accidentally, the commitment and expectation shifts to adhering to the plan rather than wholeheartedly participating in the reality of the experience. There might be an amazing opportunity that momentarily captures your imagination... that becomes a lost possibility in your rearview mirror as you zip along to your targeted and timed destination.

I can't fool you. You know this is true in its actual application as well as a metaphor for the whole of your days. Flexibility is that sweet intersection between preparedness and informed openness. Sprinkle a little unexpected meandering in there and you really have something! You've heard this sentiment lots of different ways: "If you don't know where you are going, ANY road will take you there." I want you to know that if you are SO precisely clear on the way to get to your target, you might just blink while you zip past that life-changing adjustment to your prepared map.

Be certain to keep your eyes open. And pretty often look left and look right. Don't miss destiny on a hurried clip to your destination.

Love,

Your Life

While planning our first month-long road trip out West and along the coast, we'd scheduled our lodging for each night. The route was solid if not overly ambitious. We'd fly into Vegas and drive to Seattle then on to Portland and down the coast of California to Los Angeles with a stopover at the Grand Canyon before returning to Vegas for the flight home. When my Aunt Sylvia got wind of our trip, she and my uncle invited us to spend the night with them in their RV in Grady, a tiny, out-of-the-way, northern California town they would be visiting for an RV rock hound caravan.

Aunt Sylvia was my magical aunt. For years, when she visited on Christmas night, she arrived dressed up as Mrs. Claus, complete with tiny gold-rimmed glasses perched at the end of her nose. She made a point to stay until she'd read everyone's tarot cards. What that had to do with Christmas, I'll never know but it was a tradition cherished by all who attended. Aunt Sylvia was the first person in my family who offered up unconditional love when I came out at twenty years old. She made time for the two of us. With four brothers, there wasn't much room for "girl time," but she created space whenever I saw her.

How could we not make room for a visit on our month-long trip?

It wasn't in the plans. We pulled out the map. Grady wasn't anywhere near coastal California. In fact, to make the brief visit, it meant rerouting a significant portion of the trip. What to do? Accept the invitation and adapt the map.

When we arrived in Grady, they greeted us like celebrities, introducing us to everyone in their RV caravan. Several people invited us to join them in crafting rock jewelry, patiently teaching us how to use various grinders to transform plain looking stones into works of art. We listened to dozens of stories from the open road and laughed together.

That night, my aunt and uncle took us to the best Mexican restaurant in town. They offered us a couple of nights in their home in Walnut Creek just outside San Francisco and made us swear we'd visit the Jelly Belly Factory along the way. Later, when we bedded down in the RV on the sofa turned double bed, I fell asleep listening to their harmonious snores. Before heading out the next morning, they fed us and handed us bag lunches for the road. We hugged and posed for pictures, taking a few of our own. They are the last photographs I have with my aunt. Three years later, just two months shy of a visit to our hometown, she was killed instantly in a highway accident in that same RV.

> " When given the opportunity, love adapts the map.

Looking back, I believe that love had a hand in our visit to Grady, California. Love allowed our hearts to say yes when our heads vehemently wanted to say no. I am grateful beyond words for those sacred hours, shared laughter and sweet memories. When given the opportunity, love adapts the map.

Try This:

1. Over the next week, notice any resistance to stray from scheduled activities when necessary. Ask yourself, what might happen if I adapted the map?

2. When it comes to love, find a way to adapt the map. Even if you can't say yes, think of another way to use your love superpowers. Example: "I can't pick Susy up from school, but if someone drops her off here, I'm happy to keep an eye on her until you get back from your meeting."

3. Stretch your willingness to adapt the map. Actively seek opportunities to participate. When friends or family invite us to dinner at the last minute, unless we are under a tight work deadline or have designated the time as our couple night at home for the week, we tend to say yes. Part of showing up with love is participation. These together times with others often bring us all closer together.

4. Stretch even further. A couple we didn't know particularly well invited us to their wedding on the beach. It would have been easier and more comfortable to decline but we accepted the invitation. The wedding officiant turned out to be the head of a local nonprofit. We ended up attending the reception, held in a funky café called the Cajun Bayou and closed down the dance floor that night sharing every dance with the wedding officiant. When the band took their breaks, we talked. Our willingness to adapt the map birthed some referrals but more important, a deeply treasured, life-long friendship.

Are You Okay?

You cannot do a kindness too soon, for you
never know how soon it will be too late.

—Ralph Waldo Emerson

Dear You,

I check in with you all the time. Yes, that's Me. I
make sure it looks like a stranger, or a bird or a
feather in your path, or your dog. Really it's Me
asking you, "Are you okay?"

That refreshing wind that comes at the perfect
moment? Or the scent that the wind carries to
remind you of that sweetest of memories? Or how
about the time last year when you bit into that
dessert I had sent out unexpectedly and you said,
"THIS tastes exactly like my childhood." That was
ME. I'm not trying to get kudos or extra credit by
telling you this. I'm telling you to assure you that
I want to look out for you. Check in with you. Put
my hand on your shoulder with the assurance of
presence. With just three words you can do the same
for others: "Are you okay?"

Practice it today—let me know how it goes.

Love,

Your Life

When we tumbled from our bicycle one morning after being side brushed by a truck, traffic continued to zoom past. We were hard to miss. Our tandem recumbent bike is over eight feet long and the two of us lay sprawled on the ground in neon yellow jerseys and spandex shorts. This wasn't some freeway. It was a two-lane road filled with drivers itching to get to work.

For several minutes no one stopped. Not. One. Person.

Finally, after we'd had plenty of time to assess ourselves for cuts, scrapes and bruises, after we'd had time to roll our heads from side to side and gingerly begin to stretch one arm and then another making sure everything was in working order, one lone car pulled up. The driver was our undercover love angel. She rolled down her window, leaned out and with a face full of concern, asked two questions: Were we okay? Did we need help? She may have offered to give us a lift. But by that time we'd ascertained we could get home under our own power. It might take us a while, but we could do it.

It wasn't that we needed a lift. It was simply, in that moment, we needed someone to care, to love on us just a little bit because we had scraped our knees, fallen (and falling isn't the same once you pass a certain age) and frankly, were shaken up as much by what could have happened to us as by what did happen.

We thanked our angel and with our insistence, she drove away, but not before delivering exactly what the doctor ordered—loving kindness.

Mary Anne adds:

Patti Digh has schooled us in a way of making this inquiry what we use and really appreciate. It's just a different way of noticing what is happening in your immediate world and making a tender inquiry. She uses the example of a parent in a public place with a child who is differently abled. Sometimes a child with a different way of relating to the world will have a meltdown, right in the middle of aisle seven. There are all kinds of ways that the public responds to such an event ranging from judging to intervening too much. The suggestion is to say, "This looks hard. Is there anything I can do to help?"

It's important to notice her distinction. "This looks hard." That brings you closer in to the circumstance. Saying, "That looks hard," sets you back from the experience. One word and it conveys a significant difference. It's important to wait after you ask the question, and it is good to resist the impulse to offer a multiple-choice list of suggested options. Just respectfully ask and if the parent says, "No thank you," accept her assessment and carry on.

Try This:

1. Simply practice noticing what is happening in the world around you. Put your phone down and tune into others. Look at the faces of those around you. Notice the expressions. Who might need your brand of loving kindness?
2. Be ready with an instant, heartfelt, "Are you okay?" We don't check in enough with others. We don't want to pry. People need to know that someone cares enough to ask, "Are you okay?" Be that person for others.
3. Pay attention to co-workers and those you spend the most time around. If you notice that something seems off, just ask, "Are you okay?" Be prepared to listen.
4. If you see an accident happen, pull over. Ask, "Are you okay?" Ask, "What can I do to help?" Sometimes it's making a phone call. Sometimes it's offering reassuring words. Sometimes it is holding someone's hand while waiting for the first responders to arrive. I'll never forget the young woman who stopped when my brother was seriously injured after being thrown from his motorcycle. She held his hand and talked soothingly to him until the paramedics loaded him into the ambulance.

Chapter Eight:
Champion Others Regularly

In everyone's life, at some time, our inner fire goes
out. It is then burst into flame by an encounter with
another human being. We should all be thankful
for those people who rekindle the inner spirit.

—*Albert Schweitzer*

Dear You,

Champion. The word calls to mind some historic
figures. Larger than life champions. That could
include a picture of you.

To champion—a verb available to you all ordinary
day long. It often shows up alongside heroic actions
and attitudes. When you speak up on behalf of a
cause? SHE CHAMPIONED EQUALITY. When you
speak up when someone has been poorly treated?
HE CHAMPIONED FAIRNESS. When you decide
to go to work to dismantle systemic racism? THEY
CHAMPIONED SOCIAL JUSTICE.

You can be a champion every day. Being a champion,
being a hero, is usually something that sneaks up
on you. Rarely do you wake up thinking, "This is
my day that I've scheduled to be heroic." When an
immediate need is visible and you have the impulse
to meet it (even, perhaps, without being aware that
you also have the skill) that is the intersection where
heroism is mapped. So. Champion on!

Love,

Your Life

Tama finished reading the last few words of the beginning of my book draft and looked up. "This is good. I mean it. This is really good. Just keep going."

I blushed. I wanted desperately to hear those words, wanted to soak them in, wanted to own them but wasn't ready to claim the title of writer. Not just yet. But her words kept the seed of belief alive. I would write tomorrow and the day after that. I would keep writing.

Later on, Mary Anne echoed Tama's sentiments but went even further, insisting I acknowledge the writer she saw in me. When I moved too slowly, she upped the ante, announcing the existence of my social media presence to her fans before I'd made my first post. Mary Anne knew that for me to claim the title of author, I'd have to hear it from others, knew I'd have to own it by showing up. Without her firm push from the nest into the world of online publishing, I'd still be writing for an audience of one.

Champions don't just feed us what we want to hear; they tell us what we need to hear. They push us, knowing that often our greatest fears are simply roadblocks to the best version of ourselves.

Many of us need to hear, "You can do this." How many of us crave just one person who recognizes our seed of talent or goodness? How many of us need that final push?

Others are waiting for your encouragement, your challenges, your kick-in-the-pants championing. What are you waiting for?

Try This:

1. When a friend or relative announces they are going to try something new, tell them, "I believe in you." Chances are, they're recovering from the discouragers. In the beginning, you may be their only champion. Ask them about their dream. What motivates them? When they lose sight of that dream, hold their vision up for them. Remind them how important it is. How does it feel to show up as a champion to others? Journal about this.

2. Ask a friend who is starting a new venture how you can support them. Then listen to their response. Maybe they want you to share their Facebook page or invite your friends to their first open mic night or babysit one night a week until they get their dream off the ground.

3. Put your money where your mouth is by supporting someone's dream. Help fund their first album by donating to their crowdsourcing campaign, purchase a set of their first greeting cards or attend their first public performance. Even small gestures matter. Perhaps more importantly, reinforce for them your belief in their dream. Journal about the investment you are making in other people's dreams.

4. Champion someone you don't know. Visit a crowdsourcing site. Choose a project that touches your heart or something you wish you dared try, and contribute, even if it's only a dollar. Consider it your cosmic championing gift to the planet. If you want to stretch, do this weekly. Just imagine all the dream seeds you'll water with love! How does championing others impact your own life? Journal about this.

Make the Case/Use Your Voice

You have the power to raise others up, to use
your voice for good in the world. Use it.

—Marci Moore

Dear You,

Unless you have lived under a rock (and I know
you haven't) you can at least sing the first words
to "We are the Champions." My friend, You are. A.
Champion. You know when it is essential to speak up
on your own behalf. And, always a little easier, when
to use your voice on behalf of others.

It's a case of being a role model. You teach others how
to treat someone who is different by allowing them
to see you exercise acceptance. You make the case for
more equitable treatment by providing it yourself.
And, close to home, you teach others how to treat you
in the manner they observe you treating yourself.
Respect within and respect emanating outward. To
use your voice on behalf of yourself or others does not
imply belligerence or disrespect. Do not hesitate to use
your voice on behalf of the good of others. Or your
own good. Making a case for someone else's good can
be delivered softly. It might be delivered forcefully. It
can be delivered fiercely. There is not a single way to
correctly be a champion. You can feel confident that
the impulse toward and exercising your capacity to
be a champion is always correct. Go. Make that case.
Use your voice. You might even consider humming
that familiar tune under your breath! Who can you
champion?

Love,

Your Life

You have the power to raise others up and use your voice for good in the world. When I first launched *Show Up with Love*, Mary Anne Radmacher introduced my work to her widespread community—before I even had a social media presence! She asked her followers to keep an eye out for my work. Pam and I rushed like madwomen to create a web presence and began posting my words coupled with Mary Anne's beautiful artwork. It was simultaneously exhilarating and nerve-wracking. Mary Anne's bold introduction brought attention to my work that might otherwise have gone unnoticed or gained traction at a much slower pace.

Later on, I paid Mary Anne's gift forward by posting a request for guest artists. Painter Anita Skow responded first; photographer Mary Meares joined in next. Their visually stunning artwork serves as the backdrop for many of my essays and aphorisms. Using my own platform, I introduced both of them to different audiences than they already had. When you share other's writings or gifts within your network, you are using your voice to raise their visibility. You are making a case for their work in the world.

> *When you share other's writings or gifts within your network, you are using your voice to raise their visibility. You are making a case for their work in the world.*

Patti Digh, renowned author and speaker, uses her voice to remind us that we are all naturally creative. She acknowledges that while we may have dismissed our creativity or buried it under mounds of adult responsibilities, at our core, we are still creative beings. She wants us to reclaim that inborn creativity.

Patti put action behind her words when she launched a creativity camp for grownups that introduced a wide range of creatives to one another. Through Life Is A Verb Camp, Patti uses her voice and the voices of other inspiring creatives to help attendees courageously jumpstart, reignite, or deepen connections to their passions and creativity—whether it is through music, knitting, painting, writing, drawing or something else. Since launching camp, she has fashioned a community of creatives who eagerly encourage one another and other emerging artists.

Both Mary Anne and Patti regularly use their voices and platforms to speak out against bullying and to stand up for and alongside those who have been bullied.

You don't have to be famous to use your voice for good. Pam is an extraordinary connector of people. She studies individuals, remembers what's important to them and fearlessly connects them to one another, companies and causes that she believes in for the ultimate betterment of society.

You, too, have the power to raise others up and to stand for goodness in the larger world. Use it. When you discover someone with a gift, tell everyone you know. When you feel compelled to stand up for a cause, use your voice to positively influence others.

Try This:

1. Look for the excellence in others and share it. Once you discover excellence, tell your friends. Tell the world. When you visit a new restaurant that excites your taste buds, tell everyone you know. Share it widely. When you discover a new author, poet or play, spread the word.

2. Ask someone you admire, "How can I help you get the word out?" They will tell you. Trust me. Some of us are a bit on the shy side. Maybe we're not experts at marketing and could use a little assistance. Ask how you can help.

3. Use your voice, your platform and your connections to spread the word. Be bold. Your boldness might rock someone's world and change the world for good in the process.

4. Take action. Patti Digh made what she calls a Strong Offer to support fellow creatives. She said let's gather and learn together. She issued an invitation and asked others to spread the word. They did. She has rolled out offers of camp for several consecutive years now consistent with her original impulse, increasingly championing the skills and connection of those participating. As a result, hundreds of creatives have blossomed. How might you use your voice and your talents to raise others up? What actions are you willing to take? Spend some time journaling about this.

Nurture Spirits

Nurturing is not complex. It's simply being tuned
into the thing or person before you and offering small
gestures toward what it needs at that time.

—*Mary Anne Radmacher*

Dear You,

You'll notice that Life rarely just does one single
thing. There isn't a single seed in a seed pod... but
many. And cones on trees. Well, you've stepped on
enough of those to get my point—lots of cones. Apply
what is modeled for you in nature to how you live
your days. If you are going to nurture one spirit,
make it plural. Two's almost as easy as one. And
three? Well, your call.

If you are going to address an envelope and write
an encouraging note "just because," to a friend you
miss or someone who is not well, or in an extended
recovery (or serving overseas, or... the list could
become extensive so I'll stop now), consider making it
plural and doing two. If you hold the door open for
one stranger, consider holding it for a few others. The
smiles and comments you'll get will make the plural
effort worth your while.

Nurturing spirits is an act of planting seeds in the
garden of someone else's life. You rarely get to see the
harvest of effort... however you can be certain that
there is a harvest that will likely continue on for
more seasons than you could initially suspect.

Love,

Your Life

The first time Grace called, I was stunned. It's not every day that I receive a call from the other side of the world. In her lilting voice she semi-shouted, "Marci, this is Grace from New Zealand! You don't know me but I read your Facebook posts." For the next forty-five minutes she shared her perspective on love, supporting others and then talked about her mission—knitting and distributing individualized prayer shawls across the planet.

When moved by the circumstances of others, whether it is the loss of a loved one or a friend in need, she tenderly crafts prayer shawls with love-inspired colors to send, shipping them wherever needed. Grace's prayer shawls have the unique ability to arrive unexpected and just in time.

I've learned that once wrapped in one of her prayer shawls, recipients feel loved, protected and supported as if Grace herself were there, enveloping them in a much-needed hug. Grace tends to a large flock across the world. Her supportive words and continual prayers on behalf of others lift them up in the most trying of times.

Grace's heart breaks at the tragedies of others. Her first instinct is to ask, "How can I best support you?" When Grace asks, you know it comes straight from her heart. She listens deeply then asks clarifying questions. Afterward, Grace offers one or two nuggets of wisdom—short, powerful and on target. Yoda-like in those moments, she only says what needs saying.

By paying attention to what is happening to those around us, like Grace, we too have the capacity to be just in time nurturers. I watch this regularly play out in social media. When a family recently experienced a medical crisis, an online friend launched a crowdfunding page to help cover their whopping $12,000 insurance deductible.

Donations poured in. Those who couldn't donate offered expertise or crafts for sale as incentives for donors. Local friends ran errands, grocery shopped, delivered dinners and babysat while the mom stayed by her son's side through multiple surgeries. Messages of support flowed in as well as toys, games and homemade videos designed specifically to keep her young son entertained.

Championing others often looks a lot like nurturing. Look for opportunities to nurture others, both in and outside of your usual circle.

Try This:

1. Nurture people with your presence—even if it's driven by tech. There's nothing like a friendly face saying, "We're behind you all the way" or "I know you can do this."

2. Nurture people long distance. While I was working on the book, various people nurtured me long distance. They'd ask how the book was going and really listened. The encouragement I received from others moved me beyond measure. During the last week when I set myself a pretty tight deadline, co-author Mary Anne sent brief, sometimes five-word notes—just enough to keep the fire going.

3. Nurture others by being there—really being there—when the going gets tough, as it does from time to time. Remind them, "You've got this and I'm here for you." When unexpected neck surgery put me on my back for quite a while, my mom came each afternoon to sit with me. She is a nurturer of the highest order. She didn't ask to make conversation. She brought my meds when it was time, made sure I ate what little I could, made sure I was comfortable and checked on me while I slept. She quietly cheered noticeable progress. Between Pam, Mom and our assistant, someone was always there for me. Friends, camp buddies and the Radmacher Project Team stuffed my mailbox with cards throughout my healing. One person sent a humorous card nearly every week—always when I needed a good laugh. That's just one example of how "being there" matters. Your nurturing and your championing make a huge difference.

4. Nurture one another with old-fashioned caring. One dear friend champions us by asking, "How are you doing?" It's as if she has a sixth sense, a special knowing about how our lives are going from more than a thousand miles away. She'll ask point-

edly, "How are you taking care of yourself?" She knows we can't change the world if we work ourselves into the ground. She's a big proponent of rest, good food and exercise, preferably outdoors. If she weren't close to our own ages, we'd probably call her Mom. Everyone needs at least one of these—a champion who can lift you up *and* keep you grounded in what matters.

Be A Mirror

It is an absolute human certainty that no one can know his own beauty or perceive a sense of his own worth until it has been reflected back to him in the mirror of another loving, caring human being.

—John Joseph Powell

Dear You,

It's a common recommendation in business communication training when someone explains or expresses something to you, you then get to say in response, "Let me repeat back to you what I've heard you say so that I can be sure I got it right." That is being a mirror.

When you are a mirror to another you have the capacity, rather than giving them what you want them to have, to reflect their truest need and provide that very thing. That is being a mirror.

Being a mirror takes a concentrated effort to look at the person, listen to their words, attempt to grasp their body language. If you want to shake things up a bit you could just admit what you are doing, "I am going to act like a mirror and hold up for you what I just saw."

See how that goes for you—and them. I'm warning you, though, people can be startled by what they see in a mirror!

Love,

Your Life

Mary Anne Radmacher shares these experiences:

I told a longtime friend, Gina, that a true heart recognizes the same in others. A longtime human rights activist, she explained a concept she'd learned in her work in refugee camps. We talk about the heart as the seat of compassion and connection. In Africa, it's the liver. Yes, they'd say, "He's captured her liver." Regardless of the body location that we identify, we recognize a kindred spirit from deep within us.

Experts in communication encourage people to listen hard, from a deep place, and then "mirror" back to the speaker their understanding. In fact, it's such a common practice, people can get a little cheeky with the familiar phrase, "Here's what I hear you saying... " In spite of that, the practice is solid. We mirror each other whether we intend to or not. We know people whose state of being influences the room they are in. "He lights up the whole room the second he walks in." "She can suck the air out of the room." Both assessments are unintentional mirroring of another.

When Love controls the mirror, we hold it up to others in many different ways. If you have ever said of someone that they are able to help you see things more clearly or that they seem to know you better than you know yourself, you have experienced the amazing quality of a person acting like a mirror. The key to this mirroring is the capacity to notice.

A mirror is a reflection. A repetition. A return back of what is set in front of the silvered glass. There is wisdom in this reflection. Kathleen Gallagher Everett often says, "We reward the behavior we want to see again." That applies to those around us and to our own selves. What if we began noticing feelings of love and contentment, satisfaction and reward, ease and enthusiasm? Noticing trains us to be able to duplicate that which produces positive outcomes. "I see how you handled that difficult customer. It was gracious and swift and the outcome was really ideal." You are serving as a mirror by reflecting to that person behavior that deserves to be noticed and that you would enjoy seeing again.

The mirror also works in the reverse. Seeing and taking note of the things which cause discomfort, drain, dread... provides the opportunity to change the circumstances that led to those states and experiences.

Try This:

1. Practice listening hard. Hold the impulse to offer a solution, or interject your own experience until you are certain the person is done speaking. Asking "What serves you best here? Do you want me to listen and hold your words safely? Do you want me to respond from my own experience? Do you want me to mirror back to you what I have heard and seen as you were sharing?

2. Practice being an accurate observer and listener. When you reflect what you've heard, attempt to be concise, without personal commentary. A mirror reflects.

3. Once you've reflected back to a person, make space for their response. Your willingness to be a mirror, your message of "I see you and I hear you," often opens room for authentic, rich conversation.

4. Continue to come from a place of curiosity. Elaborate on this concept of curiosity. You can always say, "Tell me more" or "What does that look like?"

Chapter Nine:
Give from the Heart

The best way to find yourself, is to lose
yourself in the service of others.

—Mahatma Gandhi

Dear You,

You often have the impulse to share, to give. That
calendar of yours shows lots of occasions to give
someone a gift and there's always the gift that is given
just because, "This made me think of you."

The business practice of offering "free gift with
purchase" puts a twist on the heartfelt portion of
gift giving. What is offered in this context is a sales
incentive, a premium upon purchase. You have to
buy something to get something.

Giving from the heart is not like that. Giving from
the heart is one of the times that you do not want
any strings to be attached, even if they are "heart
strings." A gift with a string attached can get yanked
back to the giver in so many ways. You've had it
happen to you. That far away relative for whom an
annual visit means pulling all those gifts out of the
closet because you know he will ask about each one.
("Did you ever find a good use for that ____ I gave
you a few years back?") Giving that is accompanied
by a ledger sheet is more like something that broke
right after you bought it, but you get charged
interest on it, year after year.

Giving from the heart means it leaves your hands
and it is no longer yours. It is the property of the
person to whom the gift was given. Anything else
really can't be called a gift and is more accurately
referred to as an obligation. Or even a loan.

THIS might be pretty important to remember: Just

because someone offers you a gift does not mean you have to accept it. And, conversely, if YOU are giving from the heart and someone doesn't want to accept... please understand THAT gift was a gift likely better intended for someone else, not them. Rather than letting that hurt your feelings, get right to work noticing who is actually supposed to get that gift from your heart!

Love,

Your Life

Generosity shows up through kindnesses, service, words, and gifts for strangers and loved ones alike. There are as many ways to give as there are people to think them up. You don't need to limit yourself to what you've been taught. Your natural creativity and care for others will serve you well.

Five days before Christmas, a young man walked up to a holiday market vendor finalizing her booth for the starting bell. He opened a box to reveal a pie tin with three pieces still inside and asked, "Would you like a delicious piece of pecan pie?"

"Why don't you save those for yourself?"

Smiling, he said, "I bought the pie just to give the slices away."

I loved that act of showing up with love, spontaneously walking up to people with a love offering. His mission wasn't to change the world. It was to simply be generous—not to give someone what they needed but to bring a smile to their hearts and their taste buds, to give them a taste of receiving from a perfect stranger, with no strings attached.

Susan makes a point of finding the best bargains on gloves and blankets. She stockpiles these items in warm weather knowing she'll go through every single one during the first cold snap. Susan has a real passion for serving the homeless. She's one of those individuals who lives to make the lives of others easier.

A few minutes into the keynote speech at the Gluten Free Living Conference, a baby started crying. Several audience members turned and stared at the mother. When the baby continued crying, several more people turned, some glaring. As the little one's cries turned into wails, the mother hurriedly gathered her things, placed the baby in the stroller and began pushing it toward the exit.

The speaker stopped mid-sentence and looked directly at the mother saying, "You don't have to leave. You are not bothering me... or any of us. I am probably bothering her. Please stay." And with that he picked up where he left off.

One Christmas, a few short years after we'd officially met Pam's bonus family, we received our usual box of Christmas pecans and a Christmas card from her uncle. When we opened it, a check fell to the floor. When we picked it up and saw the amount, we cried.

It was beyond extravagant and completely unexpected. It was a gift we'll always remember. It was the first time we'd ever been the recipient of such generosity. We were stunned and filled with gratitude.

He couldn't possibly have known the perfection in his timing—or maybe he did. I'd been away from our business for much of the year dealing with a rotator cuff injury and providing emotional support to my brother who'd been diagnosed with ALS.

Here's another example of extraordinary giving. Mary Anne remembers:

In a period of financial uncertainty, it became clear that I required a car for my work. My household referred to the 14 year old van we shared as the "mobile dog kennel." It was dependable enough to get to the dog park and back home. Through a series of negotiations that I learned about afterward, my partner was negotiating the purchase of a used Prius from friends of mine. While it was the car I hoped to have—someday—it fell outside my budget at that time. After some consideration, I proposed a payment plan and a strategy to get the car across the country.

Caren Albers shares her perspective on this accounting of generosity:

When I gifted our used Prius to Mary Anne, I gave it fully and completely, expecting nothing in return. The kicker was, I got as much joy out of giving as she did in receiving it. Believe me, that's saying something because she was thrilled!

I was a little surprised when Bob said that Mary Anne's partner had expressed interest in purchasing the Prius. We live in Florida, which is a continent away from Whidbey Island, Washington, but I was intrigued.

Opportunity knocked, and her partner had answered, and now we all wondered if this thing had legs? Could the car be relocated to the Northwest? After the initial conversations through Facebook

Messages between the men, Mary Anne emailed me. She said that a pre-owned Prius was her dream car and her husband was quite enthused. She proposed a payment plan that fit with their financial needs but claiming the car involved both a long wait and a drive across the country. She was pleased that we came to a workable agreement.

But my heart had other things in store. The more I thought about it, the more I knew in my heart I wanted to gift the car to Mary Anne. I could tell it would make a world of difference in her days and life. Now, accomplishing this in a way that lifted her spirits as well as mine became the goal.

Two days after our initial agreement, I told her how happy it would make us to be able to express our generous spirits in this way. We were so excited to help someone, and at the same time have our dream car become someone else's dream car. It was the most perfect outcome we could imagine.

One of the most important things to do when giving a large gift is to ask the person if they are open and able to receive it. And she had a big task because we were planning on giving her the car and making sure it was delivered to her. Both as a gift.

I sent an email message to Mary Anne, so that she would have time to experience my request privately first. I asked "Would you be open to receiving the Prius as a gift from us? No strings attached. I already know you love me! It would be a gift to us, too. Consider it a return on the good karma and the positive energy you share with the world." My email ended with "We would be thrilled if you would accept. Let me know where your mind goes on this." I only know because she told me that after her initial gasp, and momentary disbelief she broke into what my friends and I like to call, "The big, ugly cry."

What has transpired since then is the amazing, uplifting power of this gift to change both of our lives. She's had access to a reliable car with excellent fuel efficiency and has been able to travel the Pacific Northwest in service to her work. Knowing that she travels without concern about the safety of her vehicle makes us both so happy.

Gifting has so many edges that we bump up against not the least of which is resistance to accepting the gift. Mary Anne could accept with joy what others often cannot. She accepted with grace and joy and I know that she trusted the love behind the gift and understood that we were letting go with our heart. I'll keep giving, we both will, no matter the result, because giving fully, hitting a bulls-eye on the target and truly feeling the magic of helping someone, does my heart so much good.

Try This:

1. Begin seeing yourself as a generous person. Even if your bank account has three figures instead of four, five, six or ten, what might you be able to give? Look in your pantry. Are there a few items you could drop off at your local food bank? Do you have an hour to care for a neighbor's child? Can you bake something for the school bake sale? Can you give someone a bus token or a lift? Say yes to one small act of generosity this week. Make a note in your journal about what you were able to give and how it felt.

2. Look for opportunities to give from the heart. Who might need you to accompany them to a doctor's appointment? Who might need a shoulder to lean on? Who might need a gas card more than anything else in this moment? Who might need your time? Offer your assistance to at least one person.

3. Find a way to use your specific gifts in giving to others. The Rad- macher Project invites members to send uplifting notes or cards to those who most need them. Groups such as the Rotary and the Lions club offer members many ways to serve. Habitat for Humanity is always looking for volunteers to build homes. How might you use your special gifts to enhance the lives of others?

4. Expand your definition of giving. Continually scan your envi- ronment for opportunities to give. Create a giving bucket list. If you won the lottery, what organizations or individuals might you help? Hint: Your list just might give you a clue about where your giving priorities lie. Where can you make a dent, beginning today?

Give to Causes That Touch Your Heart

If you can't feed a hundred people, then just feed one.

— *Mother Teresa*

Dear You,

Whoa. Isn't there a lot of need all around the world today? It can be overwhelming. If things are kind of tight in the bank account right now, you might be tempted to think that you are not able to give to causes that touch your heart. Currency is so much more than money: It is a matter of energy, time, goods, sharing information, teaching, volunteering with a needed skill set... that's just the short list! I am confident you can think of many more ways that you can contribute. There are people in tough places in your neighborhood and all the way on the other side of the world. Weather, error, accident, harm are all fountains requiring filling. It's easy to be overwhelmed by the scope of hurt and need circling the globe. Pay attention, when your tender heart can bear it, to the causes and events in the world that are in alignment with your calling and heart. Contributing to those causes according to your abilities—the what and the how—will return graces and rewards to you in unimaginable ways. Just listen to your heart.

I want to assure you, I write these letters to you because I love you, not because I expect you to write back or because I think you are a "cause" of any sort. Besides, even if you wanted to write back, I don't have a post box!

Love,

Your Life

Give when you can, where you can, how you can. Your gifts change the lives of others and, along the way, just might change your own.

My parents introduced us to generosity early on. My brothers and I tithed ten percent of our meager allowances, often under duress, to the churches Dad pastored—sometimes even more for special offerings, saving up our change in containers the church distributed for such purposes. Then there was our meager supply of playthings. On Saturday mornings, at Mom's request, we rummaged through our toys for ones to give to neighboring children who didn't have any. And in the evenings, we offered up prayers for the safety of missionaries serving around the world. I consider myself fortunate to have been raised in a family deeply committed to the wellbeing of others.

These early experiences taught me two lessons: one, not to form deep attachments to my belongings, and two, that no matter how little I have, I always have more than enough to share with others, even if only a whispered, heartfelt prayer.

Giving is incredibly personal. If your daily mail looks anything like ours, each week you receive multiple solicitations for deserving nonprofit organizations. As much as I know each has a worthy mission, we cannot act on every request.

For years we wrote dozens of small checks to many organizations but more recently decided to focus on heart-centered giving in four distinct areas: hunger, human rights, gun safety and increasing opportunities for disadvantaged youth.

We support cancer research because it lengthened the life of Pam's Aunt Carolyn with cutting-edge cancer trials and because cancer touches far too many lives, including my own. We support both local and international food organizations that focus on eradicating food insecurity so that children don't go to bed hungry. We give to Big Brothers Big Sisters because not every child experiences the opportunities and level of support our nephews enjoyed growing up. We've seen firsthand the impact positive adult role models have on children. Finally, we give to human rights organizations because all humans deserve equal rights.

We give out of gratitude and out of hope. We give to make a dent in the unending well of need.

Try This:

1. Connect with your compassion. When you read or watch the news, what catches your attention? What moves you to tears? What puts a walnut-sized lump in your throat? What makes you think someone ought to do something? Make a list. Make contact. Offer what you can whether it is service, funds or both. No contribution is too small.

2. What criteria might you use for your giving list? Ask friends and family what causes they connect with and why. Ask how they decide which causes to give to. What criteria is important to you? Must the organization be local? Must it be financially healthy?

3. Create your personal giving list. Your list becomes a measuring stick for how you will give both time and money. These days, when I receive donation solicitation calls, I can honestly reply, "Thanks for the opportunity but we already give to Big Brothers Big Sisters." Fill in that same blank with where you focus your giving.

4. Commit to giving consistently. We've made promises to give. People and organizations count on our gifts. Remember what it feels like to receive a paycheck or retirement check each month? Nonprofit organizations need that kind of security too. Once you find a cause that fits your measuring stick and touches your heart, commit to some amount, even if it's five dollars per month. A few years ago, we made a pledge that we ended up extending later on. I admit to being nervous committing to that kind of donation over a period of years but not once have I regretted it. Knowing that we regularly contribute a portion of our resources toward bettering the world is an investment we can live with. How about you?

Let Go with Your Heart When You Give—Let a Gift Be a Real Gift

Generosity is love.

—*Lailah Gifty Akita*

Dear You,

What happens when "going the extra mile" turns out to be a much longer journey? You cannot always predict the measure of an impulse toward generosity. You can prepare the heart for grace; you can set down expectation and just respond to whatever comes next. If the unexpected journey of giving starts feeling like there is a string attached that you feel inclined to pull on—that's a sure sign to you to re-visit the reason behind your giving.

When you give, if it's a physical thing, your hands have to let go of it in order to give it. You also get to let go with your heart. That's how you can tell it's a real gift. So, back to the length of any giving-journey, know that you'll go until you stumble over a string that you inadvertently attached somewhere along the way. If you don't trip, but you do start mumbling… maybe something that sounds like, "This isn't exactly what I signed on for," that's another sign that your heart is holding onto something that would be better if let go. When you are clear on the boundaries of your own capacity, you can participate in open-hearted giving. And(!) there ARE maps for those long, unexpected journeys! They are all titled beginning with the same word: Love. Look carefully: In addition to all kinds of routes and ways to get to a place… you'll see boundary lines, too!

Love,

Your Life

A close friend was diagnosed with a life-threatening illness. Based on her religious beliefs, she opted against traditional treatment. When Linda first told me, I wanted to get on my knees, take her hand and beg, "Please do everything you can to get better. The world needs you. I need you!" I wanted her to live, wanted her to fight with everything she had. Instead, with a single hug she knew I deeply respected her decision though I would never truly understand it.

Despite the illness spreading across her cheek and pressing down into her mouth making her speech difficult to understand, she continued working full time, continued showing up at community events and continued changing the world for the better.

Well-meaning friends offered advice along with best treatment options. When Linda explained her alternative treatment decision, some scoffed. Others walked away unable to accompany her on the path she'd chosen. What Linda most wanted was loving support and an unconditional acceptance of her decision. Those disagreeing with her lifelong beliefs only compounded her distress.

As we have over the years, Linda and I scheduled a breakfast date. When the day arrived, I felt frightened that I might burst into tears, wouldn't know what to say or might not be the comfort she needed. The little girl inside wanted to stay home with the covers pulled over her head, already pre-grieving her friend, but the big girl, fighting tears, dressed and went anyway. Her illness had spread. A new growth threatened to close one eye but after two minutes of sitting across from one another, everything fell away. Love replaced fear. All I saw was my friend.

We ended up visiting for almost three hours that day. The longer we sat, the more Linda opened up about the challenges her illness presented: the way people refused to look at her, how, even in her presence, friends often asked her husband how she was faring instead of addressing her and how others simply disappeared from her life. She talked about feeling invisible but focused more on her latest adventures and plans for the future—none of which involved slowing down. I opened up to her more than I had in the past. We spent the hours as two longtime friends—deepening what already existed.

During the last two years of Linda's life, we shared many hours together. At first, I took her to upscale restaurants, wanting to create memories and offer some sense of normalcy. Over time, as Pam and I learned to let her lead, Linda taught us to give in ways that nurtured her. We frequently visited her at home, bearing soft foods or milk shakes. On most nights we huddled like teens on Linda's L-shaped sofa while she regaled us with stories from her lifetime. Laughter filled the room as did occasional silence. As her illness progressed, we told the stories or talked until she dozed off.

Today we treasure these hours for what they were—precious gifts of togetherness and unconditional love—her way.

While it would have been far easier to send cards and flowers, what my friend craved more than anything was time, friendship, heart-to-heart connection and regular doses of normalcy. Anything less would have broken her heart and filled me with a mountain of regrets. Fear hesitates. Love acts. Be there when it matters most.

> *Fear hesitates. Love acts. Be there when it matters most.*

Try This:

1. Before you purchase your next gift card, reflect on what you know about the recipient. Based on your knowledge, what might be a gift that would soundly resonate with what *they* care about or like? There is nothing like receiving a gift that abundantly shows the giver knew exactly who the recipient was at their core.

2. Grow your ability to deeply notice and make note of clues your friends share about what's important to them. Give those things. When someone tells me they've always wanted to take a cruise, I jot it down. While I can't give them a cruise, I can give them a gift card toward a cruise. Once, after a particularly tough long-term consulting gig, Pam's mom and her sister gave us spa gift cards. They were paying attention. Create your own cheat sheet. When friends mention interests or express wishes, record them.

3. Put your listening heart on. What do those in your life most want? How can you make that happen? Linda let us know that visits meant the most. And chocolate milkshakes. And goodbye kisses on her cheek that said I love you dearly. One evening, on our way out the door, we asked her husband if there was anything else we could do. He shook his head and said, "Keep coming; just keep coming." Honor your friendships with gifts of love.

4. Let them lead. Find out what others most want. How? Ask. Linda was pretty clear. Be here for me. And we signed on, come what may. Ask what your friend wants and do your best to accommodate it or find someone who can. For me, as long as it's not illegal or immoral, I'll do my best to make it happen. Text, call or write. Bring them their favorite cake. Pick up their kids from school. Take them to Disney World. Drive, take a taxi or fly. Find a way to show up their way, even if it's a stretch for you. Remember, it's not about you. It's about them.

Offer Compassionate Service

A kind gesture can reach a wound that only compassion can heal.

—*Steve Maraboli*

Dear You,

When you offer compassionate service, remember something important. The offer is the first act of service. It might end there. Perhaps the person rejects your offer with a sturdy, "No." Accepting that answer is a peculiar part of being in compassionate service. Your second act of compassionate service comes when you receive a "Yes." You control the service you are offering, not the yes or the no that you will receive.

When you receive a YES to an offer of compassionate service, celebrate what you are able to do. Perhaps you will want to continue making offers. Or, perhaps this one act of compassionate service was exactly what was needed and nothing more. Doing what you can, when you can, is sometimes all you can do! Be gentle in the offering and know that even the simplest of compassionate gestures are enough.

Love,

Your Life

Our friend, Kathleen Gallagher Everett, cooks up compassionate service and explains the recipes with a sweet sense of humor. She shares:

For generations women have supported each other through difficult times. Some rush to the side of the friend in crisis, giving generously of their time and good advice. Others drag the miserable one out for a much needed night of dancing and play. When I hear a friend's bad news, I head straight into the kitchen to tie one on—an apron, that is—hoping I'll be able to say with butter, flour and sugar what I can't put into words.

"Suzanne, I am so sorry to hear about your mother. Here is a loaf of cinnamon bread. I kneaded it in my little kitchen where the windows face east so the sun and the bread could rise together this morning. She seemed like a really nice woman. I'd love to hear more stories about her when you're ready to tell them. I hope you like raisins."

"Aimee, I am shocked that he left you for the dental hygienist. I don't have the name of a lawyer to give you, but I did bring you a casserole. I'm naming it, You're Too Good for That Jerk Chicken. It goes really well with cheap merlot. You won't feel bad forever. I promise. Call me before you do anything drastic."

"Cheryl, no one will think that guinea pig died of neglect. It was nice of you to volunteer to take care of it over the break. I'm sure the teacher will understand. It was probably about 108 in human years. Here are two dozen Cheer Up Chocolate Chip cookies for strength while you deliver the bad news. Try to save a few for the kids."

"Edith, I know the chemo might affect your appetite, so I filled your freezer with containers. Six of them are You're No Chicken Soup, with plenty of nettle, prayers and garlic in it. The others are ravioli I shaped into hearts for when you need a reminder of how dearly loved you are, and it comes with unlimited refills. You will be well again."

When Angela across the street called to say that her brother had a stroke, I headed once again to the kitchen, this time to make a basket of food and a thermos of coffee for the long ride ahead of her. I expected she would drive straight through the 700 miles and not stop for meals. And knowing Angela, she'd be crying all the way across Ohio, so I put extra salt in the egg salad to make up for all those tears. While I packed, the cell phone in my apron pocket delivered a text message from my daughter: "Samantha's boyfriend broke up with her—do you think I should make lavender cupcakes or a nutmeg torte?"

A new generation, another woman, amassing her own collection of recipes for disaster. During challenging times, friends need friends who deliver cosmic casseroles with a heaping side of love— without being asked. Be that kind—delivery guaranteed.

Try This:

1. What is your typical response when you hear of a friend going through a challenging time? How do friends know you care about their concerns? Take ten minutes to journal about how you respond and then, if there's room to expand your response, how you might want to respond in the future.

2. In challenging times, friends need friends who deliver cosmic casseroles with a heaping side of love. What's your specialty? If you don't have one, what might you deliver to cheer someone up when words are difficult to come by? I'm not a cook but I'm a pick-up artist when it comes to take out. I've delivered vegan food, Thai food and on-demand milkshakes. I specialize in sending comfort in whatever form it looks like for that person.

3. How might you love larger when it comes to friendship disaster response? List your natural gifts. Are you an organizer? Might you offer to take charge of meal deliveries or scheduling visitors? Are you the social media queen? Might you offer to keep others posted on your friend's progress? Are you the baker of the group? Might you offer to hold a baking party to stock your friend's freezer? How might you use your natural gifts to make a difference in the life of a friend?

4. Commit to providing your own brand of disaster response to friends in need. Plan for how you will respond to local friends versus long distance friends. How will you consistently show up with love?

Chapter Ten:
A Little Help from Your Friends

I would rather walk with a friend in the
dark, than alone in the light.

—*Helen Keller*

Dear You,

From deep in your belly your voice rises. You can
as easily sing harmony as you can melody. You are
content singing by yourself—a solo. In fact, you often
sing when no one else is around. You sing, and your
heart listens. Your heart knows the crystalline cadence
of your lovely voice and it knows also the richness of
joining with other voices. At the end of the matter,
some of the best performances come from allowing
other voices to join with yours. Just because you can
sing alone, doesn't mean you have to. The best bits of
this grand musical of your life come when you let
yourself be a fully engaged member of a chorus.

There's that whole "go it alone" mentality and doing
stuff your own way. Sometimes that's the best choice.
Sometimes it's the only choice. But I'm pretty sure
my friends, the four distinct seasons, agree: Things
go better when working in cooperation with others.
Can you imagine what would happen if Winter
suddenly decided no help was needed from the other
three seasons? It's not pretty. Accepting cooperative
assistance is a sign of strength... and the results are
often multiplied in really dynamic ways. Almost
every adventure is improved by holding the hand of
a friend.

Love,

Your Life

Life takes a village... of friends. I wasn't sure just how many I had but when my brother Mark was diagnosed with ALS, the number of friends who reached out to help surprised me. We don't have to manage life alone; sometimes we need to raise the flag of surrender saying: I quit pretending to be superhuman. I welcome your assistance.

There are two times in my life when I remember being profoundly moved by the depth of love and caring inherent in friendship. Once was at my dad's funeral service. As people spilled into the church for Dad's service, friends made their way to the front to hold and comfort me. Clients we'd done business with for years sent not just flowers, but staff.

On the most difficult day of my life, friends fiercely supported me in ways I never expected. And, as many times as I've shown up for others, I never understood at a heart level the gift of presence—the delicate web of support that comes with no expectations. I didn't need to be anything other than what I was in that moment—a little girl missing the man who helped bring her into the world, a new member of the exclusive club no one wants to join: those who've lost parents.

The people encircling me at that moment were, in many ways, extensions of my own family. I will remember that moment as the epitome of how it feels to have so many others show up with love for me.

The other was the day of my legal marriage to Pam, followed by our reception. Pam and I married in the state of Washington. One couple flew in for the ceremony and the other already lived there. As the six of us entered the tiny glass chapel in the middle of nature, we gathered, unrehearsed, in a semi-circle around the minister. One member from each couple added their blessings.

> *On life's journey, friends are Spirit's boots on the ground, loving us through our deepest sorrows and dancing beside us in our greatest joys.*

The atmosphere filled with such love and intimacy that at times, we all held hands, deepening the existing connection of friendship.

Back home, another dear friend—one we met on the

146

dance floor at a mutual friend's wedding—opened her home for our reception as her gift to us. Friends crowded in, the din of celebration rising. As I looked around the room, I noticed many of the same faces I'd seen at Dad's service, a testimony to friendship at its finest—unconditional love.

On life's journey, friends are Spirit's boots on the ground, loving us through our deepest sorrows and dancing beside us in our greatest joys.

Try This:

1. Purposefully befriend others. We often sit on the sidelines thinking *pick me, pick me*, but don't always reach out to others the way we would like them to reach out to us. This is particularly true for introverts. We hope someone notices how fun or smart we are and makes a point to get to know us. Others are often waiting for the same from you. How about we meet in the middle? What if you start reaching out? Stretch your inner circle to include new friends.

2. Pay attention to what is happening in the lives of your friends. Check in often. Your friends won't always let you in on what is happening, perhaps because they don't want to overburden you. One friend asked to schedule a date for lunch. Our schedules were overloaded from too many clients and not enough rest. We begged off. Several months later, when we finally came up for air, she admitted her husband had left her and asked for a divorce. I was flabbergasted, and deeply apologetic. I'd let my friend down by not showing up when she needed me. At the end of our call, I said, "Please, please, please, when something huge is happening in your life and you need my attention, say it." I took her lunch meeting request as a simple chance to catch up. She was asking me for a lifeline.

3. Make it a point to be there, in spirit as well as in person if possible. One friend emailed back and forth with me over the two days we were losing Dad. Beyond Pam and the rest of my family, she walked through that journey with me as much as any other person there. Her loving words, straight from an angel's heart, kept me afloat, gave me the strength to walk back into his hospital room and do the next difficult thing.

4. Celebrate the milestones in the lives of others. Be there with enthusiasm. Presence means everything—whether it is in spirit or at the event. Let them know how much you love them. Give a toast or write your loving thoughts on a note and mail it; let them know how thrilled you are for their joyful occasion.

Be a Neighbor, Not Just a Resident

It's very important to know the neighbor next door and the people down the street and the people in another race.

—*Maya Angelou*

Dear You,

Maybe you do not know the person who lives right next door to you. Is the clerk you see every day a neighbor? What about that face you recognize at the post office?

You and your neighbors connect in all kinds of ways. Maybe it's just a friendly smile you offer the person who lives down the street. Maybe it's something as out of your comfort zone as starting a neighborhood watch program or an emergency contact tree. I know you can think of several ways to become more rooted in the place you call home right now.

How large is your neighborhood? Can you expand your idea of neighborhood? The global community, connected in so many digital and actual ways, provides a different kind of way to "borrow a cup of sugar" from your neighbor.

Give it a try today. Be a neighbor where you live, not just a resident.

Love,

Your Life

When I was a child, the moment a new neighbor moved onto our street, Mom welcomed them with a smile, a hearty casserole and some of her famous chocolate chip cookies. Today we might consider that behavior intrusive, except it isn't. It's an offer of friendship. And if we choose to shut ourselves off from those invitations, we are failing to show up with love. It's quite possible the person offering you something needs something, too. Maybe your neighbor is not only showing up with kindness but looking for some in return.

We have a neighbor who finally moved back to the States after retiring from teaching overseas for most of her life. I worked from home at the time and if Amy caught me in the front yard or out at the mailbox, she'd stop to chat. Her visits weren't always conveniently timed and at first, I battled impatience, especially if I was working on a project or just yearned to get my introvert self back into the house, but Amy became my teacher. Instead of hurrying through conversations, I learned to breathe, settle in and let the visit run its course. She rarely hurried. She had her priorities: her dog, her neighbors, her meticulously kept home and yard, volunteer work and arranging flowers—a labor of love.

I thank Amy for teaching me how to show up for my neighbors. I began heading to her yard when her dog was outside—an excuse to play fetch as well as visit. In the beginning we limited our conversations to safe topics: the weather, changes in the neighborhood or Blake, her trusty Springer spaniel. She asked questions about our work, curious how we were able to stay home so much. She once wondered aloud if we were independently wealthy. I assured her we're not—just blessed to regularly work from home. Over time, Amy's questions went deeper, got more real.

At some point, I found myself asking bolder questions, too. As our conversations turned more personal, I learned Amy had a daughter who lived far away. She listened as I talked about my older brother's struggle with alcohol and later on, his journey with ALS.

Over the past few years we've become her surrogate Florida daughters, welcoming her into our larger family and attending her annual Ikebana flower events. We bring Amy treats from our travels and give Blake Christmas gifts. In return, Blake sends us cards for every holiday on the calendar. When we travel, Amy keeps an eye on our home as if it were her own. She once even called our local paper to stop delivery until we returned! She keeps us posted on anything relevant to neighborhood happenings and has introduced us to every other doggy parent in a five-block radius. Amy is as invested in our lives as we are in hers—all because of a series of conversations she initiated.

Our visits transformed my heart into that of a neighbor rather than just a resident—once I made the time to listen. Someone in your neighborhood might be waiting for you to open the door.

Try This:

1. Look for openings to connect with those in your neighborhood. Look receptive to conversations. Pay attention to your body language. Make eye contact, smile and wave. Noticing and commenting on home or yard improvements are risk-free conversation starters; pets are, too.
2. Regularly spend time in your front yard or walk/cycle in the neighborhood. We've met far more neighbors this way than by staying in with our windows closed. While we don't know every person's name, we know the name of their dogs or how many kids they have. We know enough about their habits to know if something is amiss and we need to check on them.
3. Offer your assistance. Amy's dog, Blake, is energetic and loves to run. By showing up and playing fetch, I give Amy a break. If you are dashing to the store, ask your neighbor if you can pick something up for them. Helping once isn't a lifetime commitment; it's simply being a great neighbor.
4. Create a gathering for your neighbors. Whether it's once a year or once a month, a block party, porch party or backyard barbeque offers neighbors the opportunity to become friends.

Bonus Try This:

Journal about your experience as a neighbor. How receptive are you to friendly overtures from your neighbors? How do others know you are open to being a good neighbor? When is the last time you've welcomed someone new into the neighborhood? How important is it for you to be a good neighbor?

Remembering and Celebrating Milestones

Those who joyously celebrate milestones in the
lives of others weave savored memories into the life
tapestries of those celebrated. Weave, baby, weave.

—*Marci Moore*

Dear You,

You live among wonder masquerading as what
you are used to seeing. You utilize technology that
was beyond imagination just a blink of time ago.
You might impact or influence a child today who
will grow up to govern amazing cultures or create
unimaginable inventions.

If there's a skill you have been working a long time
to master and you finally finish that project? Party!
If someone you know went back to school years
after being away from the classroom and is going to
graduate? Celebrate!

Psst. Don't make this general knowledge, but some
weeks just making it to Friday is worth a little
festivity. Know what I'm saying?

Notice how powerful your life is, use your tools and
your technology in a way that allows you to celebrate
it, mark it, and live into it, owning that power and
the moments that reflect that power.

Love,

Your Life

Birthdays rock. So do retirements, anniversaries, weddings, graduations, bar mitzvahs, adoptions and births. These occasions grow sweeter wrapped in the well wishes and loving thoughts from friends and family.

Choosing to celebrate significant milestones in the lives of others sends the message they most want to hear: You matter to me, I support you and I love you.

When Pam and I finally legally married, those who wholeheartedly participated during the ceremony and celebrations that followed forever etched themselves and their love on the walls of our hearts. As congratulations poured in, we realized what we'd missed out on during our previous eighteen years together: the enthusiastic acknowledgment and support of our relationship by others. Celebrations matter.

For Mom's seventieth birthday, the family threw her a surprise party. It wasn't fancy. We held it in a church hall that we decorated the night before. We served cake, punch and light refreshments but mostly what we served up was love—by the bucketful. As Mom's friends, former colleagues, students and out-of-town relatives poured through the doors that Saturday afternoon, she gasped, hardly believing all the people who showed up to celebrate her special day.

> *Celebrating with others gives us permission to say I love you or this is what you've meant in my life—before it's too late.*

For the next two hours, completely impromptu, attendees took turns sharing their personal recollections and connection to her. No one shifted in their chairs restless to get out the door. They stayed to hang on each word, as did we—honored to be part of this celebration, not simply of her birthday but of a life well lived.

Celebrating with others gives us permission to say I love you or this is what you've meant in my life—before it's too late. Mom's seventieth birthday gathering allowed others to inundate her with love just as she'd done for them over her lifetime. Though Mom turned eighty last year and we managed to surprise her yet again, the birthday she still marvels over is her seventieth.

Celebrations are sacred acknowledgments, pauses that help us momentarily prioritize the important over the urgent. Your exuberant participation is welcome and appreciated, a gift to those being celebrated.

Consider making a habit of celebrating other people's milestones. No matter where your friends or loved ones live, show up in your own special way on their special day. Make the call. Send a card, flowers, balloons or a gift. Make it personal—from one heart to another.

People won't remember every detail of their lives but they will remember those who celebrated their joys.

Try This:

1. Keep all-occasion cards handy. Make it easy to celebrate the important occasions in other people's lives.

2. Engrave birthdays and anniversaries on your calendar—in gold. Then take action. Send a card, flowers or a gift and if possible, show up in some way. Call and sing happy birthday or your own special song. Find your own way of keeping up. Pam and I set aside time toward the end of each month to sit and write cards. We note the date to send each card out on the back of the envelope and put the cards with other outgoing mail.

3. Add celebration events to your calendar as soon as you receive them. Plan how you will respond. Attend if you are able. Otherwise, a personal note tucked inside a celebration card means the world. Every so often I revisit our wedding book, reading the well wishes, still stunned by the people who reached out immediately with enthusiasm, congratulations and offers of assistance.

4. Show up in person, if at all possible. Even if it's inconvenient, even if it's right in the middle of your usual nap time or interferes with your regularly scheduled massage, show up. Attend with enthusiasm. Go early and stay late. I still smile at the thought of our friends, Linda and John, dancing nonstop alongside us until the DJ finally turned off the music after our commitment ceremony. Needless to say, they nestled even deeper in our hearts that evening than they already had.

Comfort in Uneasy Times: You've Got Love

Never underestimate the lingering effects
of a dash of spontaneous comfort.

— Gina Greenlee

Dear You,

It's weird, isn't it? Somebody you care about is going
through an uneasy time and it ends up freaking
you out. You aren't going through the uneasy time
yourself, but you are experiencing anxiousness over
what to do for the one who is. You worry about how
to best comfort them. And for all your over-thinking
and fussing, I could have saved you the trouble. You
already have exactly what they need: love and seeing.

One of the best things you can do for someone going
through an uneasy time is offer them comfort by your
witness. Acknowledge that you see that what they are
going through is hard. Difficult. Perplexing. Let them
know you see them. You see the hard thing they are facing.

And then the other thing is love. That person you
care about has a problem—they are not a problem.
Let them know that you love them. In the midst
of hurt, not in spite of hurt. Hard times come to
everybody, you know. You had a turn. And, I'm
pretty sure you'll have more turns. Just having
somebody see you in your rough spot is a comfort.
Add love to that equation and you've got Comfort
with a capital C.

Know you don't have to fuss so much. The answer to
"What can I do?" is simple. See them and tell them they
are loved. If they need more from you, those two things
open the door for them to ask for what they need.

Love,

Your Life

Our friend and fellow camper, Laurie Foley, offered her best advice on meaningful comfort during an extremely challenging time. She shares:

Ever since I was diagnosed with advanced ovarian cancer, people have asked how they could help me or someone else they knew who was in the middle of a hard situation.

I have one answer that I offer every time: Send text messages.

There was certainly a time that receiving that tip would have surprised me. I was committed to the idea of the grand gesture. However, there is a reason that "the road to hell is paved with good intentions" is a cliché: It's true. Or, at least it's true for me. I'm embarrassed to admit how often my sincere intentions have not translated into action.

I'm not knocking grand gestures. For me and my family, the grand gestures felt like a love bomb had gone off. Hand-crafted cards, healthy meals with special treats for my son, tokens of the heart... they all helped me and my family feel deep love. The love bomb helped to counteract fear. It absorbed sadness. It helped me learn very quickly how to live and love in the moment. The love bomb was a huge gift and a welcome distraction from the terrifying diagnosis.

But when the dust had settled from the initial love bomb, it was and is the simple text messages that are tremendously sustaining.

"I'm at the grocery store. Do you need anything?"

"I saw your husband earlier today. I just want you to know that I am thinking of you."

"I think this is the week that you are seeing the doctor. I hope it goes well."

"Text me back if I can give your son a ride later today."

"Sending you a hug."

It is like the old AOL voice saying "You've got mail." Except the voice in my head that accompanies the ping of an incoming text says "You've got love."

A text message is about as small a gesture as possible, but it makes a big difference. Mother Teresa said "It's not how much we give but how much love we put into giving." Supporting someone in a crisis is not about scale. Simple acts of love are cherished even in the hardest of times.

An extended illness or any chronic challenge is a marathon that can be tremendously isolating. Thoughtful texts connect us and sustain relationships when visits or even phone calls could feel draining. Text messages are the loving spritzes that are often exactly what we need to feel refreshed and restored.

Who would you like to feel the ping of "You've got love" today?

Try This:

1. Remember back to a time when you have felt especially comforted. What made you feel loved and held by others? Journal about what you remember. What stands out for you about the experience?

2. Comfort others by asking what comfort looks like for them. While many people appreciate cards and notes, comfort is extremely personal. As Laurie pointed out, texts provide comfort and require little energy expenditure from the person receiving them.

3. If the person has a difficult time imagining what might comfort them, give them two or three options of ways you can offer comfort. This takes the onus off of them to come up with something on their own. I can text you. I can sit with you while you are having your treatments. I can read to you from any book of your choosing. I can watch the kids while you take a nap. I can bring your favorite coffee drink and leave it beside your bed. I can loan you my favorite comfort buddy (my Curious George from childhood) until you don't need him anymore. Your list can be as varied as your skill set or your ability to pick up take-out.

4. What can you offer in the long haul? Odds are that during your lifetime, someone will need you beyond the initial love bomb. How will you keep on showing up? How will you offer comfort for the long haul? It helps to have a plan. What are you excellent at? Are you a talker? Great at just "being with" someone? How might you consistently show up in ordinary ways that say, I am thinking of you today? Journal about your responses.

Chapter Eleven: Stepping In and Stepping Back

Sometimes love is knowing when to step back as
much as it is knowing when to step in.

—*Marci Moore*

Dear You,

I know it's odd to think of doing nothing as doing
something. And yet, nothing is occasionally exactly
what is required. When someone you love and care
about is in harm's way, or hurt, or recovering, you
want to go and DO things. I get that. I really get it.
Take winter, for example. A lot of people think that
I'm just kicking back, doing nothing in winter. It
looks that way. Dormancy is pivotal to the riot of
color and bloom that happens in spring. Without the
apparent "stepping back" of winter you'd never have
the Maypole dance stepping-in of spring.

Even if someone invites you into their hurt, or their
grief... consider that one of the highest gifts that
you can offer them is your "nothing." No doing. No
talking.

No fuss around food or errands or processing mail
or answering phone calls. Just sitting there. "Doing
nothing." I guess what I'm saying is know when to be
winter.

Love,

Your Life

Just two days after we buried Dad's ashes, doctors admitted Mom into the hospital, suspecting a stroke. Fortunately it wasn't, but the thought of suddenly losing her, after just having lost Dad and my brother within the past month, terrified me. Pam and I moved in with Mom. Initially we tiptoed around, overly cautious not to be a bother or get in each other's space, enough so that we ended up not supporting each other the best way we could. As the first week spilled into the second, Pam invited Mom to walk in the evenings. Each night Pam would come back and share some of the things they discussed. With the back-to-back losses she'd suffered in addition to her own health scare, Mom needed mountains of TLC—Tender Loving Care—plus time to grieve and begin to find her way again.

We fell into a comfortable rhythm of life together: planning meals, cooking, taking walks, talking at the end of each day and listening to her stories of life with Dad. Mom particularly enjoyed our twice a week mother/daughter lunch dates. I listened as she sorted through her loss and the almost fifty-eight years my parents had spent together. The longer we stayed, the more Mom relaxed, opening herself to the nurturing and comfort her family offered.

We began taking her on small outings and tried to make sure she had something to look forward to. One Saturday, after we'd returned to our own house for a few hours to catch up on chores, we checked in to see if she felt up to going out. She jumped on the idea. We picked her up and took her to Ted Peters, a local watering hole famous for its smoked fish. Once we'd been seated, she announced, "I've always wanted to go here but your father would just say no and keep driving." Neither of us could believe she'd never been. Our waitress served up gigantic platters of smoked fish with all of the fixings. We shared another house specialty, a frozen mug filled to the brim with root beer. Afterwards we drove out for a sunset walk along the beach.

My brothers showed up in their own ways. Joel and his family began taking Mom out for lunch after church. Marvin would swing by to make repairs around the house or spirit Mom away on adventures. Paul routinely called from Washington State, and flew home, devoting his days to the two of them hanging out together. Little by little, Mom began to find her footing, create new routines, make friends and get out with people. She began to discover her own interests, eventually returning as a volunteer chaplain at the Tampa International Airport and as a new volunteer in a thrift store.

We're all still there for her but in a different role, more on the fringes. Just as parents who watched their children grow up and go off to college, we've moved home and backed off, giving her the room to find and redefine herself. As much as we wanted to make her life perfect after Dad passed away, we had to let her grieve and grow on her timetable. Sometimes love is knowing when to step back as much as it is knowing when to step in.

> *Sometimes love is knowing when to step back as much as it is knowing when to step in.*

Mary Anne adds:

The rhythm of stepping in and stepping back is one that is personal, almost like music that each person plays with the actions of their life. A precious friend encountered cancer and prevailed for a long period. And then, he didn't. Prevail. And in the recognition of what seemed to him inevitable, he stepped back. Kindly. He offered a written grace to all who knew him explaining how he was going to step back into the core things that mattered most to him in his final days. Ralph Bramucci was a man who understood that balance between in and away, so well expressed in this letter which I share with you now.

Dear friends,

As you may have heard through Mary (his wife), last week we made the difficult decision to stop the chemotherapy drugs I've been taking. The medications do not seem to be stopping the growth of cancer, and when weighing the side effects, the doctors advised us to focus instead on quality of life and time with family.

With this new phase I find myself reflecting on past years, and the friendships and community that have sustained and enriched my life. I want to express my gratitude for all we have shared. Knowing you, laughing with you, building memories with you, has been a great privilege.

It occurs to me that circular patterns are part of nature's design. We are born and discover, diversify, and eventually return to a point of closure. In viewing life this way, closure is not actually the closing of a door. Rather, it is a gathering together of all we have lived, felt, experienced, learned. You have held an important place in that cycle in my life.

Celtic Christianity contains a concept of thin places. A thin place may be literal—a mountaintop, a place in the wilderness, or more experiential—music, writing, silence. Whatever represents the thin place for us, it is something that gives us a glimpse of the holy, the divine. You have all represented a thin place in my life.

I am focusing on time with my family right now. Mary and I are enjoying having the three kids and our new granddaughter here with us. I may not be able to respond to your individual emails and messages, but please know that you hold an important place in my thoughts and reflections.

With affection and warmth,

Ralph

In this way, Ralph made his love for his extended circle clear. He clarified that the way to express love for him at that time was to respect the boundary he was placing around himself and his immediate family. This echoes Marci's view—love steps in and sometimes, love steps back.

Try This:

1. Make your strong offer and let go of the outcome. Patti Digh defines a strong offer as making an opportunity available without being attached to the outcome. We didn't insist on moving in with Mom; we asked if she would like us to stay for a while. She gratefully accepted.

2. Know when to call in reinforcements. I asked my brothers for specific types of ongoing help, once, and they responded beautifully. Fortunately, three of the four remaining siblings live within minutes of one another. You may need to explore what resources are available in your area. One friend enlisted a geriatric specialist to help her navigate the challenges with siblings during a parent's decline into dementia.

3. Keep the lines of communication open. We asked Mom on more than one occasion if she was ready for us to leave. We assured her that we were completely open, either way. We knew it was time to step back when she finally said, "I'd like to try this on my own for a while."

4. Look for evidence that it's time to step back and do so, when necessary. Sometimes, even when the person wants you to stay, it's not healthy for you or them. Do gut check-ins with yourself. Talk with a trusted friend or counselor if you want to explore your options. When you are on the other side of the equation, know how to ask those who care to honor your need to step away.

Love Within Borders:
Second Chances

We all make mistakes, everybody should be given a second chance.

—Lailah Gifty Akita

Dear You,

I heard you when you were upset: "That's the ABSOLUTE LAST TIME I'm going to tolerate letting them pull that stunt!"

And then, after a little time and perspective, you connect to the good you want for that person and you give them a second, second, second chance. Only your heart can tell when you are being your wholeheartedly loving, opportunity-giving self, or if you are lacking an appropriate border.

The whole forgiveness thing aside, there are boundaries for very fine reasons. It is important to self-care that you set them and honor them. Since they are YOUR borders, your boundaries, you are the only one to know when it's okay to cross them. You know. It's not anyone else's right to choose to compromise the borders that you have established. You are the only one who knows if it's another second chance, if it's a last chance or if they happen to have run out of chances. All you.

Love,

Your Life

We needed a new housekeeper, someone trustworthy to maintain our home and our sanity when intense client engagements and erratic travel eroded even the simplest of routines. When we advertised on Craigslist, one woman's response stood out. I took the precaution of looking her up online and there, from another state, was a mug shot. I read the accompanying story and Googled several others. Still, something made me pick up the phone and call the woman. Yes, she instantly admitted, it was her in the mug shot. Yes, she'd been accused of this crime but added that she had an attorney who was fighting the charges. He felt certain they'd win. She openly discussed what I'd already read. The company she had worked for shoved her forward as the fall girl, perhaps pegged her as someone who wouldn't fight back but Sharon* knew she'd done nothing wrong.

I invited her to the house for an interview. Something told me she was a good person with tremendous integrity. Since no traditional employer would hire her, Sharon found herself taking on numerous odd jobs to make ends meet. She provided a list of references for people she had worked with since the incident. We talked for a long time that day. I saw a caring woman in a tough spot in her life. We agreed to give it a try, knowing full well that once she was cleared of all charges Sharon would resume work in her chosen profession and I'd start my search all over again.

During the year Sharon worked with us, in addition to her normal housekeeping responsibilities, she aided in my recuperation from rotator cuff surgery, kept me supplied with ice packs, handed out medication when needed and watched out for me, allowing Pam to run our business single-handedly. I found Sharon to be one of the kindest, most thoughtful people I'd ever known. She apprised us of each court appearance. When she was finally cleared of all charges, we celebrated together. She left us a card that I still cherish. In it she wrote, "When I was going through one of the toughest experiences of my life, you took a chance on me when few others would. I can never thank you enough."

The truth is, I can never thank her enough for opening my heart even wider than before. Giving Sharon a second chance was as

> **And I would hope someone would take the time to see the true heart of us and give us a second chance.**

much about us as it was about her. Although friends questioned our sanity for inviting someone into our home who could end up going to jail, I stood my ground. It's entirely possible that what happened to Sharon could, through some misunderstanding, happen to any of us. And I would hope someone would take the time to see the true heart of us and give us a second chance. I would like to think someone would stand beside me, even if that someone happened to be a complete stranger prompted by love.

Try This:

1. Think back to a time when someone gave you a second chance. What impact did that have on you? If you've never thanked them, if possible, find a way to do so now.

2. Asking someone for a second chance is extending an olive branch, a way of saying, "Can we try this again?" When someone says "I goofed," and asks you for a do-over, whenever possible, say yes.

3. Think of someone in your own life who might need a second chance. How might you reach out? What would you say? Do that.

4. If there is a possibility that you might owe yourself a second chance, how might you do that for yourself? What would you say to the person in the mirror? What forgiveness and opportunity might you offer up? It's never too late to extend the same kindness to yourself.

Reach Out Anyway—Especially When It's Challenging

Do not fear mistakes. You will know failure. Continue to reach out.

—*Benjamin Franklin*

Dear You,

Working for change is begun deeply with an individual. The work of risk, the work of vulnerability and extending a hand is difficult. It takes courage. The capacity to step over fear, through resistance, and offer help, assistance, presence—these things are demanding. Ah, but you know that.

There are some people who decline help because they think that's what is expected of them. They feel compelled to look as if they are strong on their own and have it all together. Pffft. Everybody has times when they need a hand up. Other times a person can feel ashamed that they need help. Maybe it's because they need help **again**.

Here's the real point, offer it anyway. You aren't in charge of what other people are experiencing. So offer. And then, do it again. Remember that time you had the impulse to offer help—and didn't? Yeah. How's that still feel? Reach out: It's like a muscle; it builds in strength and capacity as you work it.

Love,

Your Life

The last thing I wanted to do was reopen my heart to my older brother. He'd broken it numerous times, his lifelong alcohol addiction an impassable barrier between us. At fifty, I finally washed my hands of him—completely. Even when Mom announced Mark was sober yet again, my heart remained on lockdown. I'd spent a lifetime wishing for the older brother I never had. I couldn't afford to hope again.

It wasn't until I called home from a speaking engagement in Chicago and learned he'd been struck by lightning that my heart cracked open. Hands shaking, I called the hospital where he'd been admitted.

From that point forward, we talked daily by phone and met a couple of weeks later at a restaurant not far from where he'd been injured. He was clear-eyed, funny and grateful for our visit. He and his wife seemed like newlyweds and in many ways, I suppose they were. His newfound sobriety reintroduced emotional intimacy to their marriage.

We continued our daily calls. It was during one of those conversations when he first mentioned a change in the muscles of his hand, an inexplicable weakening in his grip. During his first VA appointment, his doctor mentioned ALS/Lou Gehrig's disease as a possibility. Two months later, the diagnosis became official: Bulbar ALS. They estimated two years, give or take. I hung up the phone and sobbed. I'd done the research. Just when we'd begun to know each other for perhaps the first time in our lives, Mark was dying.

For eighteen months, I served as an integral part of his support team, spending hundreds of hours traveling between our two homes, taking him on adventures, accompanying him on doctor appointments and often visiting daily during lengthy veterans' hospital stays.

I frequently asked myself, who walks into someone's life knowing they are dying? Who dives deeper instead of running? I enlisted the help of a Hospice therapist who specialized in addiction to join me on this journey.

We made the most of our moments. Together, Pam and I took Mark and his wife on their bucket list trip while he could still talk, still get around without a wheel chair, still breathe without being tethered to a machine. That trip is what I hold onto, how I most want to remember Mark: late night storytelling sessions, laughing until we cried and his holding court at an impromptu family reunion in Virginia. Over time, I gratefully watched him gradually repair relationships with our other siblings.

Even when he began drinking again, I stayed engaged. But when he made the final mad dive back into the darkness that is addiction, when he stumbled into a place I could not follow, I finally took my Hospice counselor's words of warning to heart, "Sometimes we want more for others than they want for themselves" and backed away. In doing so, Mom stepped in, spending the last few months as a significant part of his support system.

I don't regret for an instant reopening my heart to Mark. Our time together exponentially grew my capacity to love him, others and myself more deeply. That lesson alone provided the courage to serve and to step back when that time came.

Trust your instinct to serve.

Try This:

1. Journal about a journey where love allowed you to participate even when you weren't sure you could. Think of when you have deliberately shown up in the past, even if the situation was uncomfortable. What within yourself allowed you to do that? Carry that forward when you move into the next challenging opportunity to love.

2. List five people who might serve as your support system. During the time with Mark, I had weekly visits with my Hospice counselor to help manage pre-grief plus several friends who willingly served as sounding boards.

3. Examine any areas in your life where you are called to love larger but are holding back. Journal about what you've discovered. Based on what you know, how might you reach out?

4. Trust your Source for strength, guidance and wisdom. Set aside time to connect with your personal Guide. I can't tell you how many times I prayed throughout my journey with Mark. Though my Hospice counselor was exactly what I needed, she wasn't on call 24/7. Neither were my friends. God never left my side.

Stand Up To Bullies: "It's Not Okay"

We explain when someone is cruel or acts like a bully, you do not stoop to their level. Our motto is when they go low, you go high.

—*Michelle Obama*

Dear You,

There's inherent risk when standing up to a bully. There's risk whether you are standing up to a bully for yourself or on behalf of somebody else. Because... Well, Bullies! They aren't just all bluster... sometimes they are bounce and push. Or punch. Yep. All kinds of risk.

Accountability is not a friend to bullies. A bully continues to bully because they can; they continue because they are allowed to continue to demonstrate that behavior.

To be a witness, without fear, is to disarm the first power a bully holds over you. A bully is not accustomed to being observed because fear causes most people to flee. One of the most profound acts you can do in the face of a bully is to gather yourself and others to act as witness. "I see you," has a profound impact and "I see you and I am not afraid," is even more significant. Speaking of running—gotta say—there are times when that is actually the most immediate and best option for the one being bullied. But when it isn't, remember the value of not always standing alone.

Bullies are used to operating in the darkness of their actions... When you shine a light on them and let them know you see them for what they are, everything can change. I'm here for you when you're running and when you're standing.

Love,

Your Life

Mary Anne Radmacher reflects on bullying:

Bullies operate under the mistaken belief that they cannot be stopped. Fear generated within the heart of the one being bullied might mistakenly foster that belief. Walking away from a bully, or, in some instances, running like the wind, is one of the bravest things that a person can do. Removing oneself from harm provides a host of other options. Remaining present to the bully provides a key and distinct option: Be bullied. An essential element to the structure of bullying is that they must have someone to bully—absenting yourself shifts a bully's equation.

Bullies thrive in darkness, both literally and metaphorically. Casting light on a bully is an excellent option. Calling in other light shiners is good, too. "I want you to see what I see," you can say to the witnesses. And to the bully you say, "I see you."

There is a classic Charles Schultz *Peanuts* strip where Lucy punched Linus because "he was beginning to make sense." Making a rational case to a bully is rarely effective, as bullies do not act from a rational base. You do, when you act in your self-interest and not from sheer fear. "This is not okay," is enough of an objection. Because of the complexities involved in the process of bullying it's easy to forget that part of standing up for yourself. "THIS is not okay." There.

It's true and you have declared it. Then, walk away. Removing yourself removes the fundamental requirement of a bully—someone to be bullied. You are worthy of protection.

Try This:

1. Act as a witness. If it is safe for you to do so, take a video or photograph. The process of intervening is something that each individual must consider. Quickly getting support or reinforcements often has a stronger impact.
2. Practice the art of asking others to be witness.
3. The government and many non-profit agencies provide teaching guides, local resources and talking points for those who are bullied, have witnessed bullying and for the bullies themselves. Use a reliable search engine and see what is available to you, where you are.
4. If you are or have been bullied, use the resources that are available to you to become clear of the consequences of such experiences.

Chapter Twelve:
Names, Hugs and Heart, Oh My!

If you have the grace to hug someone, never
miss this sacred moment.

—*Lailah Gifty Akita*

Dear You,

It's so cute... the way people deal with the
magnificent undertaking of telling someone else, "I
love you."

I've seen it all. My two favorites are the workaround
of stating the obvious without any personal
responsibility attached, "You are loved." And then
there's the casual toss over the shoulder, "Love ya."
That one, with even less commitment can be written,
"Luv ya."

C'mon. Come on! Three words that can change a life
or, at the very least, turn the day around. Yeah, sure.
Maybe your relative already knows. But what could
it hurt to just come right out and say it: "I love you."

"I love you." There. I said it. Now you. You go. Try.
Who you gonna tell?

Just take a deep breath. Remember all the bliss and
laughs and loyalty and look them right in the eyes
and then say the truth, "I love you."

It takes practice. It's worth it.

And I know you know. I know I just told you. But I'm
being your role model here so...

I love you.

Your Life

Love is personal. It's in the small things. It's not one or two repetitive actions; it's our willingness to dance in the moment with another human being. It's the connections we weave daily that invite one another in, just one step closer. It's the exhilarating experiencing of intentional connection.

On a cruise to Cozumel with Pam's family, we joined others on an excursion to see stingrays. Afterwards, we crowded into the ladies' room to take showers and change back into our street clothes. We sat on the long bench that stretched the length of one wall as we took turns waiting for showers to open up. A mom came in with her young son. We made small talk as she too waited for a free stall. When one finally came open, she asked if we minded watching her son while she showered. We did not. She set him on the bench and firmly instructed, "Keep your biscuits on that bench!" He nodded.

The minute her shower door shut he looked at us and declared, "I've got sand in my shoes." He then proceeded to remove them, showing off the whopping amount he'd inadvertently collected from the beach. For the next few minutes, he entertained us all. When his mom finally came out, she thanked us liberally for keeping an eye on him. We wouldn't have had it any other way.

It was a reminder of the intimacy and trust that develops between people in certain situations. We were all far from home. In those few minutes we were his extended family, a bevy of anonymous aunts, keeping a watchful eye.

Love invites us to see the opportunities in all that we do, to love unabashedly, those close as well as those in random encounters.

On that same cruise, we had a phenomenal wait staff. From the very first evening, they called us by name. The head waiter took particularly good care of Pam, making sure she had several selections to choose from that met with her special dietary needs. From them we learned it is the little things, the intimacies extended beyond our immediate families that are the icing on the cake of life.

It's hard to dislike someone you've danced with. The activity that kicked off Life Is A Verb camp was something called contra dancing. It shares a similarity to square dancing. There is a caller but there is more interaction between yourself and every other person on the dance floor. The entire purpose, it seems, is both fun and connection. Pam and I managed to stay together until the longest, most complicated dance of the night when I ended up with Keith as my partner. He is an exceptional dancer. I'd watched him float across the floor with his wife. Now he stood in front of me and extended his hand.

As often as I tried to beg out, he asked me to stay, to give it a try. Keith lived and breathed love on steroids during our dance together. He helped me feel at home in dozens of ways. He maintained eye contact and whispered instructions literally every step of the way. He loved wholeheartedly, not with a single action but a bundle of them. He was patient, encouraging and reassuring. He even changed out one motion so that I would feel more comfortable. By the end of the dance I was laughing. When I met up with Pam for the next dance, Keith's gift stayed with me as much as his willingness to stay with me during the dance.

Try This:

1. Just for today, pay particular attention to those around you. How might you connect with others you don't know or don't know well? Listen for those inspired nudges. Purposefully leave the door open for small, spontaneous connections. Journal about what you discovered.

2. Find ways to make others feel at home, no matter where you are. Befriend others every chance you get. Be the first to reach out. Even though I'm a bit of an introvert, I go out of my way to help others feel comfortable. Watch what happens when you make eye contact and introduce yourself to others.

3. Be open-hearted in familiar and unfamiliar situations. Stay curious. Move into each situation with a beginner's mind, open and ready to learn. Lean in. When Keith ended up as my dance partner, I could have walked away. I wanted to. Instead I leaned in. I gave it a chance and the experience left a lasting positive impression of what can happen when we lean in.

4. Experiment by dancing with life as it unfolds. You'll meet more people and have more lasting memories of your human experience by saying yes—even when you are slightly uncomfortable. Yes to hugs. Yes to dancing. Yes to caring about everyone you meet. Yes to other's concerns. Yes to genuine, open-hearted conversation. Yes to seeing one another through fresh eyes. Yes to discovery. Yes to letting love permeate your relationships. Some of our most precious memories rise from those temporary connections made when we close down restaurants with new friends, travel to other countries and depend on the kindness of strangers or extend those same graces to friends in the making.

What's Your Name, Again?

At my age the only problem is with remembering
names. When I call everyone darling, I know I'm
safe calling them that. I adore them, too.

—*Richard Attenborough*

Dear You,

Yes, you! You know I know your name, right? Well,
now that we've gotten that straight!

Naming someone is a Very Big Deal. Parents can
determine much of the trajectory of a child's life
by the name that they bestow at birth. There are
some folk who feel so burdened by the inaccuracy or
inappropriateness of their name that they go through
the legal process of changing it. So, we can assume
somebody's name is pretty important.

Remembering a person's name is one of the first
and finest things you can do for them. I could go
on but the point is essential and clear, isn't it?
Remember that time that the person you thought
really mattered forgot your name? That's the whole
case right there. Knowing how it feels to have your
name forgotten is the real case for working hard to
remember the names of people you meet. Give it a go.
It will serve you well.

Love,

Your Life

"I'm so bad with names."

You've heard it many times. Perhaps you have said it yourself. In an increasingly impersonal world, an individual's name is one of the only things that allows them to feel as if they are truly unique. To a child who sits in a classroom with dozens of other children, this may be especially true.

Beyond civility, or politeness, recalling a person's name is a gift. A recognition that they made an impression on you and you cared enough about them to bring their name to mind. With the speed of life, and meeting so many people, how can you remember someone's name?

Mary Anne Radmacher recalls this experience from when she was a teenager:

I belonged to a large congregation. So many people attended that the minister presented three different services. I observed something that would change the way I communicated with people. No matter what context I saw my minister speaking to someone, I noticed he addressed them by name. And often he asked about some specific current event in their life. I made an appointment with him to ask him HOW he managed that when he served thousands of people.

He told me that he learned early in his ministry that people feel anonymous. As though they were only a small cog in a much larger machine. He believed the gift he could first give to those whose souls he wanted to inspire was to assure them that he saw who they were.

Remembering names as one of the most important skills he acquired as a pastor. He gave me these valuable key points:

1. Always look directly at the person when you are first meeting them.
2. Ask their name, repeat it and even spell it. If it's a common name like Larry or Mike, don't assume you know how it is spelled. Build it into your memory by asking, "Do you spell Larry the

usual way, LARRY, or is Larry some other kind of spelling?" That gives you the reinforcement of saying their name several times, and spelling it while looking at them.

3. Ask a question that might anchor them to something you already know. "Have you been here before," "Did you come with someone I might know?" "Are you new to this city or... ?"

4. Admit at the very first meeting that remembering their name is important to you. Ask their help in the event you forget. Actually say that. "I really would like to remember you! If we meet again and, while I hope I don't, I have forgotten your name, I hope you'll forgive me and remind me." They will! He assured me that people want to be remembered and are happy to assist.

Early in my professional career, people were startled when I remembered them after only meeting them once. It's made a tremendous difference in the way I have navigated my place in this world.

Try This:

1. If you are indeed challenged at remembering names, disclose it immediately. There's no shame in not remembering and it only becomes awkward if you pretend that you do when you don't. If you are truthfully able, tell the person something you DO remember and then ask them to remind you of their name. "I do remember we had a fascinating conversation, and your name has slipped my mind."

2. Use memory devices that work for you. Ask to have a photo taken with the person and make note of their name in writing.

3. If you have time, ask the person who has reminded you of their name if they know who they were named for or if they know the origin of their name. For example, Mary means bitter in Hebrew. Anne means sweet. Bittersweet.

4. As you indicate that you are happy to speak to or meet this person, confess up front. "I'm working on improving my skill at remembering names. So next time I see you, please forgive me if I don't get it right. I'm sure going to try."

Show Up With Hugs

Hug tight. Hug often... Because love travels through hugs.

— Drishti Bablani

Dear You,

There are some childhood memories that serve you well by being forgotten. The hugs of your older self are NOT the hugs of your youth. Big people forget that simply by virtue of their size a hug to a child can be an almost suffocating experience. And if you add cheek pinching to it, and a head pat, it's the trifecta of childhood affront. I know. I've seen it. There are all kinds of ways to overcome the nose smashing, access-to-air-cut-off-all encompassing embrace. There's a whole buffet of hug types from which you can choose. I assert that even a gentle shoulder to shoulder bump can count as a hug. It's like a hug in training.

Really, all that is required of you when showing up with a hug is that you are aware of the environment. Just be observant and courteous. You might even consider asking permission before delivering your hug. You'll know: You've got great intuition. And let that intuition guide not only the type of hug... but duration. Don't worry: You'll be able to tell when enough's enough. Hugs, like all other great and loving skills, only get better with practice. So. Practice!

Love,

Your Life

Hugs often express what words cannot. Through the physical action of a hug, we often express that which cannot easily be articulated.

Dad loved to surprise us kids. He wasn't great at expressing emotions or being affectionate, but he excelled at creating lasting memories. He crafted elaborate bedtime stories and built anything we could dream up.

We certainly never lacked for adventure but everything we did was as a single group—the kids. As the only girl among four brothers, I needed something more from my dad. In my heart I yearned to be acknowledged as special and not always treated as just "one of the boys." Dad had his own way of doing things and it rarely involved words. His message to me was no exception.

At Weeki Wachee Springs you can still watch real live mermaids swim in the crystal clear water during the mermaid shows. As a young girl, these beautiful creatures with long green tails mesmerized me. I never tired of seeing them glide through the water. More than anything, I wanted to be one.

How hard could it be? For me, swimming was already as natural as breathing. We lived in my grandparents' small lakefront cottage and each year, when summer rolled around, Mom issued us our bathing suits. During those three months, the only times we stopped swimming were for meals, church or bedtime—or when lightning danced in the distance.

One weekend, on the way home from yet another full day of mermaid watching at Weeki Wachee, I loudly announced my intention to be a mermaid—not a postal carrier, a doctor nor an attorney. No. I wanted to be a mermaid. I must have said it 500 times that afternoon but with the seven of us stuffed inside our tiny blue VW bug, I wasn't sure if anyone even heard.

Several weeks later, after I returned from a grocery run with my Mom, Dad yelled for me to put my swimsuit on and come down to the lake. Right there, at the end of our long, aging wooden dock, sat the strangest looking contraption. Using his imagination, he'd pieced together a rusty bicycle, an air compressor and an old garden hose that would allow me to stay underwater as long as someone was up there pedaling away. He handed me the hose and urged,

"Give it a try." I took the hose as he jumped on the bike and started pedaling furiously.

With one look back at my dad, I plunged into the lake, stuck the garden hose in my mouth and took a deep breath. It worked! Underwater I breathed in the fresh air coming through the hose, then exhaled and repeated the process. I was a real mermaid! I swam for quite a while without coming up. I practiced smiling while exhaling and waving to my make-believe audience, exactly like the mermaids I'd seen at Weeki Wachee. I looked around without hurry, noticing the sandy bottom of the lake, seaweed floating past and some minnows darting near my feet. When I finally surfaced, I scrambled up the ladder and fiercely hugged my dad, soaking him in the process. He didn't mind at all. He hugged me back.

That summer, with his tools, creativity and a heart full of love, my dad turned a little girl's impossible dream into reality, letting her know she was, and would always be, so much more than just one of the boys. From that day forward, I knew without question that Dad loved his little girl.

Try This:

1. Examine your own willingness to hug. How free are you with hugs? How receptive are you to hugs? When has a hug been the perfect medicine for you? Journal about your experience.
2. Begin noticing when someone in your circle could use a hug. Ask, "May I give you a hug?" If the answer is no, ask, what else might be helpful to you right now?
3. Let others know that you are a hugger. Offer hugs and allow yourself the comfort of hugs from others.
4. Develop a hug mindset. You have an inexhaustible supply. Whenever possible, include hugs in your day. Share the love. Hug your kids, your significant other, your good friends and people who seem to need a hug.

Note: Hugs are typically not appropriate in the workplace. For some people, no matter the setting, hugs are not appreciated. A pre-hug check-in IS typically welcome.

Curiosity

Be curious, not judgmental.

—Walt Whitman

Dear You,

It happens at different ages... but sometime after the age of four when the most common single word out of a human's mouth is, "Why?" not knowing the answer or reason behind a thing becomes undesirable. You are built to be a lifelong learner. I'm not sure where you got that mistaken idea that you're supposed to know virtually everything at a certain age. What I do know is that the whole idea is preposterous and it messes up a bazillion opportunities to expand your perspective and deepen your knowing.

I've noticed that there is a repeated phrase among my favorite global leaders: It's "I don't know." The best leaders in the world are willing to share with the people that they lead that they do not know a thing. And even more, they proceed in asking those same people what it is that they know. The best leaders aren't so much KNOWers as they are DISCOVERers. They are deeply curious. In fact, even if they actually do know quite a bit about a thing... they know there is so much more they could know. Their curiosity leads them on that journey of discovering the more.

Do that yourself! It's some of my finest advice—be infinitely curious.

Love,

Your Life

Patti Digh shares her thoughts on learning or judging in the following:

Love or Judge—You Choose

When we encounter something or someone outside our frame of reference, we stand immediately at the edge of learning—or judging, and we have a choice to make: We can either learn or judge, but we can't do both of those things at the same time.

In an instant, we move toward curiosity ("What an interesting perspective/outfit/self-expression; I must learn more about that!") or toward judging ("How ridiculous/rude/ignorant!"). In an instant, we choose. We choose either language of openness or of reduction each time.

Choosing to be curious is expansive and generative: It enlarges our world view. Choosing to judge is reductive: It reduces ourselves and other people.

Here's a simplistic example: When I'm at the grocery store and someone moves one step "too close" to me in the checkout line, into my culturally determined sense of "personal space," I can either judge them using evaluative language: "How rude! How pushy!" or I can choose to be curious about their circumstance and cultural orientation, using that curiosity to move out of judgment. One leaves me angry and feeling violated, and the other leaves me open-hearted and generous toward another human being, with an urge toward knowing more.

Try This:

1. Apply to any decision in front of you: "I can either judge or learn, but not both. I choose to learn."

2. Assume positive intent—even if you don't believe the intent is positive. Ultimately, does it matter? Assuming positive intent will free you up from negative spiraling and keep your heart open. "That jerk cut me off in traffic!" puts us in knots. We may get angry or try to "get them back," whereas, "Oh, perhaps they have an emergency and need to get there quickly," while it may not be true, leaves us open-hearted and feeling generous toward another human being. And, really, does it matter which is true?

3. Notice your first thought and work on your second. Your first thought will almost always be judgment. This is what we do when we are unaware and faced with difference. There is no reason to feel ashamed of this—it just is. So, notice your first thought: "He's rude, she's a slob, they are thugs," and work on your second thought: "His voice is louder than mine, she might have grown up with a difference sense of self-care than me, they are exhibiting behavior that is outside my comfort zone." The first thought always shuts learning down with evaluative language; the second thought is intended to open up our curiosity about context, background, and more.

4. Choose. Judge or learn. Bad will or good will. First thought or second thought. These three decisions will lead you either to a reductive, small-hearted vision of the world, in which you feel great pain when confronted with difference, or to a generative, open-hearted way of being in the world. You choose.

Chapter Thirteen:
Off to Work We Go

If it falls your lot to be a street sweeper, go out and
sweep streets like Michelangelo painted pictures.

—Martin Luther King, Jr.

Dear You,

Even for businesses that have "Casual Friday" there
are still clothes that you have designated as "work
clothes." Then there are clothes you wear around the
house. In the hours after your work shift. Or on days
off. You don't generally wear those clothes to work.
You essentially have a uniform for the various aspects
of your life activities. Yard work. Doing dinner out.
Going to a play, a ballroom dance, a fancy opera.
These are external garments that you choose to match
your activity.

I've noticed that it's tempting to treat your loving
kindness, your patience and your sense of humor
that very same way. Like you have a YOU that is you
when you aren't on the clock and then there's the YOU
that shows up at the job. While I appreciate the work
of the human resources department trying to help
everyone behave appropriately at work, and I GET
that, there is a uniformity that should go with you,
wherever you are and whatever you are doing. Your
loving self—your impulse toward understanding and
compassion, your sense of social justice— isn't just
for the weekends.

Your ethical commitment to showing up with love
and compassion is not governed by a time clock. It's
the driver at the core of you. Now, off you go—ALL of
you—on to your next thing.

Love,

Your Life

You never know what to expect at work. Some days your work is routine; other days it may quickly become anything but. Antoinette Tuff, a school bookkeeper in Decatur, Georgia, certainly never expected to talk a young man carrying weapons and a backpack stuffed with ammo out of shooting his way through a school full of children and teachers. She showed up for work, expecting another normal day. Antoinette brought her best self to work and showed up with love.

While wrapping up this book I spent four days in the hospital. It was one of those unexpected adventures. I helped Pam lift a heavy box and felt something in my upper back give. After a couple of adjustments and one sleepless night, the badly herniated discs in my neck cried uncle. It was a holiday weekend. It was tempting not to bother with someone in pain. Over the course of two days I got passed from a walk-in clinic to the pharmacy to my personal on-call doctor to the emergency room where one physician finally took ownership. He didn't have to. He could have administered some pain medicine and sent me on my way. Instead he listened. He showed up with love. He ordered tests that could have been ordered when I first went to the walk-in clinic.

When he admitted me into the hospital where I would receive the care I needed, I sobbed with gratitude and relief. Just minutes after arriving in my room, another doctor took over. She ordered further tests and set me up with much needed medication that put my body and mind at ease. But the real angels were the nurses and nursing assistants on the floor.

Maybe it was because I was in the neuro unit or maybe it was because I lucked into the best nurses on the planet, but they checked on me constantly. They were advocates, confidants, listeners and gatherers. They protected, advised and dispensed. They were gentle. Mostly though, they paid attention to what I needed at every turn, often knowing what I needed before I did.

No matter what kind of day they'd had at home, once they walked into my room, they were completely present for me and every other patient in their care.

It made me wonder, how do we bring that same passion, commitment and level of care into our own work whether we are flipping burgers, cleaning homes, caring for patients, managing teams, designing bridges or solving world hunger?

How do we remember that our work matters and that others are depending on us? How do we stay present and give what we are able, through good days and bad? We do it by committing to show up with our whole beautiful selves, daily. We show up by looking ourselves in the mirror each morning and saying, *the world is waiting for what I have to offer. The world is counting on me.* Then we get out there and share our passion, commitment and care with every life we touch. Please join me.

Try This:

1. How do you energize yourself as you head off for work each day? How do you set your intention for what lies ahead? Do you say I have to go to work today or I GET to go to work today? Practice gratitude for going into work today and the difference you get to make in the lives of those you interact with. Journal about what you discover.

2. Your coworkers, customers and employers deserve your energy and passion. When it comes to your workplace, as in every other area of your life, you are a world changer. Your attitude, presence and brilliance are necessary components of making life a joyful journey, not just for yourself but for those who interact with you. How might you bring your passion to your work today? How would committing your passion to your workplace enhance the experience for you? For others? Journal about what you discover.

3. Be fully present at work. You have a full life. It can be tempting to let what is happening in our lives influence how we show up at work. If you've had a disagreement with your spouse or a family member, give yourself a few minutes during your commute time to calm yourself so that you don't carry negativity into the workplace. How does that feel once you've given yourself time to reset? What difference did it make in your day? Journal about your discoveries.

4. Show up ready to serve at whatever level necessary. Chances are, your workdays aren't like clockwork. You can't predict what will happen or who might need your assistance. Be ready to say yes. Journal about what needs to be in place for you to show up at work ready to be your best self.

It's Not Just Business, or Usual

We need people in our lives with whom we can be
as open as possible. To have real conversations
with people ... involves courage and risk.

—*Thomas Moore*

Dear You,

In moments of weariness it is tempting to ask, "Does
any of this (this that I work so hard toward) really
matter?"

When you return to the reason behind the start of
your work, the reminder comes: It matters to me.
And the next remembering after that is the WHY
behind why it matters to you. On the boring days.
The annoying days. The days that seemed filled with
the parts of the job that do not deliver more than a
small drip of enthusiasm, it's important to remember
the larger picture. That it matters to you, and why
it matters to you, some days, has to be reason enough.
Keep on. You'll get to some sparkly bits soon enough.

Love,

Your Life

Recently we had a show-up moment with a consulting colleague who wanted to increase the scope of her services. Since we frequently mentor newer consultants, we met at a local coffee shop and listened as she discussed different options for growing her practice. At one point she stopped and said, "Last year must have been so difficult for you with the losses in your family, moving in with your mom and then still trying to juggle your business." We nodded.

She lowered her head, then confessed, "Life is kind of crazy for me, too" and went on to explain the multiple life challenges facing her. Just like that, the business meeting turned personal. Our conversation ranged from managing clients to managing daily life, successfully divvying up our time between work, family and self-care, trying to make the best possible decisions for our loved ones and moving through life with extreme gratitude for the flexibility we have as consultants while wondering aloud what life is like for people who, because of their employment choices, don't worry about things like marketing, meeting payroll each week or choosing the best business insurance coverage.

Our conversation wasn't about solutions; it was about real life—about stressors, struggles and successes. It was about human connection and authenticity between peers.

For the next forty-five minutes we listened. It wasn't in the plan. Work waited for us at the office but this is what showing up is all about. It's about shutting off the mental timer, ignoring our watches or phones and being human with each other—for as much time as it takes. It took courage and trust for our colleague to open up to us. To everyone else in her world, she's known as the "together one"—a best-dressed, highly organized, energetic, high-performance super mom who happens to run a successful consulting practice with a smile. With us, she just got to be human. With us, she got to be supported and nurtured.

How might you further welcome authentic interactions with colleagues and co-workers? How do others know you will listen?

Try This:

1. Be authentic. I believe our colleague felt safe with us, because we'd been open throughout our personal journey with both my brother, Mark, and my dad. In the workplace, there's a thin line between over-sharing and being authentic. Model for others the kind of workplace you'd like to have.
2. Pay attention to colleagues. Notice when there is a change in their behavior or demeanor. Check in. A simple "You don't seem like yourself today" or asking "Is everything okay?" gives the other person an opening in case they need someone to listen.
3. Be open to conversations. Maybe you can't talk at that exact moment. If that's the case, let them know you genuinely want to hear what they have to say and schedule a time to talk.
4. Be attentive and flexible. Make time for important conversations. Turn away from electronic distractions, tuck your phone away and give your colleague your full attention. If you need to move to a space more conducive to the conversation you are having, do so. If necessary, schedule a time to follow up.

Everyone Can Do Something

... to the soul, the most minute details and the most ordinary
activities, carried out with mindfulness and art, have
an effect far beyond their apparent insignificance.

—Thomas Moore

Dear You,

It is a remarkable thing to stop long enough to consider how everything fits together and works together. Every animate and inanimate created thing on the Earth contributes a significance to the greater whole. There is the web of inter-relatedness in which each thing serves a vital purpose (please, please, don't mention mosquitoes. I know there's a case to be made that we could consider eliminating them. It's tempting... but I'm going to stick to my original premise). In the context of size, a gorilla far outweighs a spider. But look at the enormous web a single spider can weave. Can you imagine if a gorilla were to create a mass relative to its size, how large that would be? Huge! Everything does something to contribute to the huge eco-system that you live in referred to as Earth. Everyone has a job, a role to play. That includes you. In the trajectory of your life and in the small bits of time you call pivotal moments. Even when the weight of the world seems to land squarely on you, it really is not your job to bear the whole planet. Pick one thing. It can be a small thing. And do that. You for sure won't be able to do everything, but I know you can do something. So. Whatcha gonna do?

Love,

Your Life

When I was the Chief Financial Officer of a nonprofit organization, we received news that our budget was being slashed by ten percent. The executive director instructed me to find where we could save the money. I had the weekend to make it happen. Obviously, the money had to come from somewhere. In many nonprofits, salary and benefit costs together hover between 60 and 75 percent of the entire budget. I pored over the budget, eventually posting a large sheet with the names and salaries of every employee, searching for those who weren't specifically funded by grants.

At one point, I wanted to grab a dart and throw it at the list while blindfolded. There was no easy way to make the decisions I was being asked to make without input from others; people's livelihoods were at stake. On Monday morning I went to the executive director to discuss my findings. We could either cut several positions or reduce our benefit costs in some way, something no one, including the executive director, had been willing to touch.

> *One person, moved by love, can make a difference.*

We called an all-staff meeting. The executive director gave me the floor. I explained what had happened to our funding and how much money had to be cut. I told them it looked like some positions would have to be eliminated. And then, my own prayers were answered.

David, a long-time employee, immediately raised his hand, then stood up. He looked around at his fellow employees, then asked, "If we start contributing towards our health insurance, could we save the positions? Others nodded and looked hopefully toward me. I nodded yes and silently thanked God for the employee courageous enough to volunteer carrying some of the loss in exchange for keeping every position intact. While I still needed to work out the exact numbers, with the employees' agreement, I had permission to balance the budget without sacrificing a single job.

One person, moved by love, can make a difference.

Try This:

1. Show up. David brought his ideas to work even though they were outside the scope of what he was hired to do. He asked the one question leadership wasn't willing to tackle on their own. He was a social worker with a heart for his fellow workers. Beyond your normal job, how do you make a point to show up at work?

2. Speak up. David didn't wait for someone to ask what he thought. He had a great suggestion and put it out there. If you have something that will genuinely help your colleagues or the business itself, put it in the suggestion box or speak with someone who will listen.

3. Make every day "Bring Your Heart to Work Day." Care about your co-workers as much as you care about yourself. Find ways to show it.

4. Find your niche and shine. I excel at celebrations. A couple of co-workers and I got together to make holidays shine a little brighter for the entire admin staff. Each holiday, without fail, we crept in before others arrived and put treats on every person's desk, along with a note of gratitude. I loved hearing the happy murmurs of surprise. What's your niche? How will you help your workplace shine?

Bring Your Whole Toolkit to Work

No matter where you work and no matter what you do
for a living, you can always make a difference when
you bring your whole phenomenal self to work.

—Marci Moore

Dear You,

Bringing the whole of you—the all of your being—to
work, indeed, to everything you do, is a glorious
plan. You do not have to leave the key parts of
yourself at home when you go to work. It's advisable
that you do not; it's exhausting to split yourself up
into parts.

Living wholeheartedly means bringing your skills
and talents and abilities to work and all the places
you show up in the world. It seems easy to hold
back, to compartmentalize, reserving the funniest
parts of yourself for your friends, the creative parts
of yourself for your craft, the keen-solutions part of
yourself for your family. If you bring all of yourself
everywhere you go, you never have to remember
which parts get to go where! Take it all!

Love,

Your Life

Who are you and what unique beauty do you bring to the world? How do you take that into your workplace? If you are a gentle spirit, how do you use that to make your work more humane? If you are a fierce advocate, how do you bring that into your work? If you are generous, how does that show up? If you are creative, how do you use that in your work? If you genuinely care about people, how do you express that?

Some of us are fortunate to live our passion 24/7. Others work in jobs they tolerate for the paycheck, counting the days until they retire or find that perfect job. If that sounds like you, even now, how might you bring your whole self to work?

We recently experienced a death in the family. That alone was challenging enough but we were traveling at the time, as far across the country as possible from where we needed to be. Not only that, but we'd purchased nonrefundable tickets with one free companion pass which meant no changes allowed for the free ticket and a guaranteed change fee on top of any other charges for both.

I called the airlines expecting the worst, dreading to hear how much our revised tickets would cost. Instead, I got an angel on the other end of the phone, a customer service agent with tremendous empathy who immediately expressed genuine compassion for our loss.

She didn't have the authority to make any changes to our tickets and couldn't promise us anything at all but asked if we minded that she put us on hold so she could reach her supervisor. Several times she popped back on the line, apologizing for the length of time she was taking and again, expressing sympathy for our loss.

In a few moments she came back with great news. She'd moved our flight up to the next day and there would be absolutely no charge for changing our tickets. She even managed to seat us together on one leg of the flight and only a row apart on the next. I was and still am overwhelmed with gratitude for the young woman who did everything she could to ease the difficult journey we'd be making.

She brought her whole loving self to work. She saw an opportunity to go the extra mile and rather than blindly accept the rules, she advocated strongly on our behalf and won.

Experiences like this remind me that no matter where you work and no matter what you do for a living, you can always make a difference when you bring your whole phenomenal self to work.

Try This:

1. Think back to a time when you brought your whole self to something. What was it that allowed you to do that? Record your observations in your journal.

2. When have you felt most fully alive at work? What was happening? What was it about the experience that allowed you to feel most fully alive?

3. What skills or talents do you keep hidden at work? How might they benefit those you serve? For the longest time, I kept my sense of humor out of the workplace. Once, when we were presenting our regular conflict management program, as an experiment, I let my goofball sense of humor fly. People laughed hard and long enough that I had to stop and laugh with them. I could see the light bulbs going off and felt people connecting more deeply with the material because of the added humor. To this day I routinely bring my sense of humor to work. Even in our offices at home, if Pam's having a particularly rough day, I'll put on a silly hat, walk into her office and just stand there until she notices. Journal about the parts of you that you currently leave at home. How might incorporating them into your workday benefit your fellow employees and those you serve?

4. How might you go the extra mile for others during your workday? How might you earn the eagle award? Long before marriage became legal for all couples countrywide, our county began recognizing domestic partnerships. We went down to the court house and signed up. That little registration card gave us crucial rights as a couple within our home county. The clerk who helped us register treated us like queens. She offered to take our picture as we held up our newly printed cards. It was the first legal step that allowed us to care of each other during a medical crisis without carrying stacks of legal paperwork to prove our connection to one another. The clerk treated our registration like the big deal that it was, instead of simply another transaction. Discover your own way to transform a co-worker or client's experience from ordinary to the divine.

Chapter Fourteen:
Global Citizenship

I believe that to meet the challenges of our times, human beings will have to develop a greater sense of universal responsibility. Each of us must learn to work not just for oneself, one's own family or nation, but for the benefit of all humankind.

—Tenzin Gyatso, The 14th Dalai Lama

Dear You,

Global citizenship, when you were a kid, elicited notions of someone who traveled the world. You thought of a person whose passport was about ready to run out of room because of all the customs' stamps.

The world's ever-emerging technologies have changed all that. Now you can travel in "real time" to the most remote places on the earth from the comfort of your sofa! The perception of borders and boundaries has changed. What used to take weeks by mail now takes seconds to transmit. And there are processes in the works for some of your tomorrows that you have yet to imagine.

Global technology has created a new kind of citizenship. One that allows your tender heart to watch with delight, with empathy, with pain as events unfold on the other side of the world. With thanks to that same technology, you can act on all those things you experience. You can even arrange to go to those very places and contribute your particular skills, talents and abilities. Absent a strong impulse or the capacity to go, you can reach and support other parts of the world in so many ways. You have diverse resources and I love to see you use them. I know the country that you call home on your passport. Yet there is an address that people share... it's a simple address with just five elements:

E A R T H.

Love,

Your Life

I'd like to think that if our house went up in flames and we ran screaming into the night air, our neighbors would pour out of their homes with blankets, hugs, offers of help and more. I'd like to think we matter—that our comfort, well-being and safety matter to the people around us.

Maybe that's our role as neighbors in the larger world also—to care, to be thoughtful and to act as if everyone matters—because they do.

Never in the history of humankind have we been more deeply informed about the lives of one another, whether through live news coverage, social media or soul stirring documentaries. We celebrate, worry and grieve in near unison. We follow stories as they unfold.

Francis Bacon said, "Knowledge is power." Voltaire said, "With power comes great responsibility."

Because we know, we have a duty to act.

When a plane crashes, terrorists strike or a tsunami hits, we hear within moments. What is your immediate response? Mine used to be something like, "That is so sad." That was before the planes hit the Twin Towers of the World Trade Center, before the news swept our country within seconds, before American citizens bonded over loss, before the outpouring of support from other countries informed us that we were not alone in our sorrow, before I grasped that we are citizens of something so much bigger than the continent on which we reside.

Later, as we began traveling globally, I saw the faces of humanity and experienced our commonalities at a personal level. In Hamburg, Germany, where I didn't speak the language and desperately needed to find an open pharmacy on a Sunday, no fewer than six different people helped guide me.

In Guatemala, our tour guide spontaneously invited Pam and me to his home to meet his mother, show off her lush garden and to meet the chickens who shared their living space. He offered us a glimpse into his life. How could we refuse?

When the first plane took off from Heathrow International Airport in London after a week-long flight ban due to volcanic ash, we rejoiced with locals and stranded tourists alike. Once I understood at a heart level that we all laugh and cry, face fears, love deeply and experience the devastation of loss, I could no longer ignore the suffering of my global brothers and sisters.

Now when natural or man-made disasters occur, I immediately pray for the families of those lost or injured, the first responders and for wisdom for the decision makers involved. We are interconnected. Whether someone lives next door or around the globe, they are our fellow citizens. They deserve our compassion.

> *Even the smallest acts of kindness radiate cosmic ripples of love throughout the world.*

You inherit global citizenship just by being born. You re-earn it daily. You have a global responsibility. No matter your personal bank balance, you can make a difference. Just start where you are with what you have: Offer up prayers, sympathy, donations or direct assistance. Knit baby booties or send care packages. Support global nonprofits that can quickly put loving boots on the ground. Even the smallest acts of kindness radiate cosmic ripples of love throughout the world.

What else, as global citizens, can you do? You can always take action.

Try This:

1. As you begin your day, pause to think of those everywhere who are struggling with illness, hunger, housing, employment or loss. Send love or healing thoughts. Ask Spirit to fill their needs, heal their hearts and soften their losses.

2. When you hear news of distant tragedies, allow your compassionate heart to acknowledge the loss. Listen for inspired nudges on how to respond. Send love in whatever way you are able.

3. Start your own global impact savings account. Consistently deposit a set amount into it each week or routinely add your pocket change to your personal global aid jar. When you are moved by an event that happens outside our country, you'll have the financial capacity to respond. To my knowledge, the Red Cross and other charities don't have minimum dollar amounts for financial gifts AND you can designate how you want your contribution used.

4. Search for opportunities to positively impact the global issues you connect with deeply. Even Bill Gates specializes in how he invests in global assistance. For me, it is world hunger. It breaks my heart to think of people going to bed hungry. While I can't single-handedly solve world hunger, I can support organizations like Heifer International, Oxfam and Lutheran World Services. What touches your heart the most and how might you reach out to those who are hurting? If you have the resources, explore volunteer vacations or mission trips.

Be a Citizen of the World

I am a citizen, not of Athens or Greece, but of the world.

—Socrates

Dear You,

Perhaps the lyrics to some songs give you an incorrect impression. Love can be soft. Soft like the pillow that cradles your head perfectly after a long, strenuous day. Soft like the stuffed animal that (I won't tell anyone) you still embrace when you are feeling low or uncertain. Love certainly is that kind of soft as well as many other kinds of gentle and tender. Love has other qualities, as well.

Love is gritty. It has sharp edges. It can be compared to metal, steel wool and girders. Love can be inappropriate—showing up at an elegant party in work clothes with mud on the knees.

Great love is hard-working, long lasting and will not need to be replaced even after the warranty has expired. Love does not have a position on the periodic table; it IS the periodic table. It is the most durable, lasting, fierce element in the universe.

I want to be clear with you. Love is not only one thing. It is not only two things. It is many things and does millions of jobs every second around the world. Find just one. Do it.

And then, do that, again.

Love,

Your Life

Owning our citizenship means more than just praying, sending money or digging wells in third world countries. Being a world citizen involves daily decisions on how we use the earth's resources—everything from fuel consumption to where our food, water and clothing comes from. It's about how and where we travel and the footprint we leave on the planet. It's voting with our dollars and participating in our elections. It's refusing to purchase goods from factories staffed by children and choosing, whenever possible, to purchase goods from companies that pay a living wage. It's continually educating ourselves so that we make civic decisions born of love.

Our everyday choices, at home and abroad, have far-reaching consequences.

I learned this firsthand on a trip to Ecuador. We witnessed extreme poverty throughout, but nothing touched my heart as much as an older woman who politely offered to discard our lunch leftovers. Instead, the minute we walked away she sat down and devoured them as if they were her first meal in some time.

On the morning of our departure, I noticed three women sitting on the steps of our hotel eating bowls of soup. A staff member explained that each Sunday the women brought their own bowls and the restaurant filled them, providing a single meal each week.

I choked back tears, seeing the vast well of need with no quick fix. I thought about our role as travelers in the larger world, regretting the numerous times I'd haggled with local sellers in developing countries over a dollar or two, far less than the price of a specialty coffee at home, but perhaps an entire meal for the merchant and his family.

That day, I vowed to become a conscious traveler, a world citizen at all times. I promised to make a positive impact during each visit. Now travel is more about connection than simply sightseeing. I immerse myself in the countries I visit by learning, experiencing and participating. I make it a point to talk with everyone I meet in their language. The conversations may be extremely limited, and we may use gestures and hand signals far more than actual words, but we are communicating. Just the attempt pulls us closer together. We take turns playing teacher and student. We are equals. And that is the beauty of being a world citizen.

We are, at the very heart of everything, human beings sharing the same earth. If we want for one another what we want for ourselves—a safe place to lay our heads at night, food and access to health care—then we think as citizens rather than individuals staking our private claim. As a citizen of the world I feel a moral obligation to take the needs and concerns of others into consideration. How about you?

Try This:

1. Examine the origin of the products you use on a daily basis. What do you know about the companies you support? Are they good stewards of the planet? Do they give back to their communities or support projects overseas? Thoughtfully consider the purchases you make. What changes will you make that fully reflect your role as a world citizen? Journal about your decisions.
2. Participate in elections large and small. Study the issues and vote regularly. Research how various candidates respond beyond local issues. How seriously do candidates take their roles as world citizens? Vote in a way that not only benefits your community but the larger world as well.
3. Decide now how to increase your international footprint to naturally change the "us versus them" to "we." Commit to attending at least one or two international festivals in your own backyard. If international travel isn't an option for you, perhaps hosting an exchange student is. If feasible, encourage your children to choose mission or educational trips to other countries.
4. Plan a trip to a foreign country, even if it's on a cruise ship. Visit the behind-the-scenes areas the cruise ships don't want you to see. Talk to local citizens. Vote with your dollars when you travel. Visit mom and pop shops rather than the big-name chain stores found in many cities. Purposefully support local businesses.

Global Citizenship Begins at Home

We need to teach our children empathy and
care and love and communication and social
responsibility in preparation for adulthood.

—*Maya Soetoro-Ng*

Dear You,

Did you ever read anything by that complicated
fellow, Ernest Hemingway? He said, "Never write
about a place until you are away from it, because
that gives you perspective." I recommend that very
same thing.

We know a thing so much better when we are not
staring square at it. Having distance from the
place is a good way to develop into a global citizen.
Learn the geography. Learn the geology. Read
views from different perspectives of the history of
the place. Learn to enjoy not only the view that
distance provides physically but value the distance
across the millennia. Such views give you a more
informed understanding of any place and the people
who inhabit it. Be sure you do not allow a single
voice to inform you. The world's knowledge base is
increasingly available in so many different forms.
Taking a broader view allows you to walk more easily
in places and assume your civil and respectful role
as a global citizen.

Now, go take long, studied looks!

Love,

Your Life

Teach your children and young people that all people are created equal. Because of where they are born and where they live, they may not have the same advantages as others, but they are all our brothers and sisters. Nobel Prize winners span the globe. Humankind benefits from their contributions. Though most come from a handful of large countries, the whole of them represent nearly every country in the world. The recipients vary widely in age and their stories inspire us to be our very best.

Broaden what you listen to. Global citizenship comes with the responsibility of being informed. Read across the aisle. Don't just settle for one station as your single source for news. Your country deserves better than that. Your world neighbors deserve better than that. They are counting on you. Consider listening to the BBC, the British Broadcasting Corporation, as an additional news source. You'll become more informed on what is happening in the world from a broader perspective. You will also get a quick feel for how your own country is viewed by others. BBC has become my go-to news source when we are traveling abroad. I trust it to provide a wide range of information across the globe.

We need critical thinkers as global citizens, ones that question what they hear and what their response, if any, need be. Teach your children by word and example how the choices they make impact those in other countries. Teach them about poverty at home and abroad. Teach them what third world countries are doing to improve themselves—and what your country does to assist. Teach them how some people dedicate their life's work to decreasing poverty and increasing the health of those at home and abroad.

Depending on their age, teach them about the Rwandan Genocide and how it came to be that neighbors killed neighbors. Teach them about how their strongest allies abandoned Rwanda when the bloodshed of the 1994 Genocide began. Teach your children about the horrors of slavery and how the United States of America failed their African American brothers and sisters for many, many years. Tell your children about the heroic acts of those courageous individuals who worked tirelessly to end slavery and save the lives of slaves who managed to escape. Tell them about the president who helped end slavery. Tell them the USA still has much work to do in treating all citizens fairly. The USA is imperfect as are all countries. It is led by human beings elected by its citizens, and the history is reflective of that. The more you educate yourself and the children in your life about history, the less likely we are to repeat it.

Teach them that although all people are created equal regardless of race, religion, nationality, sexual orientation and more, many people are still not treated equally. Although LGBTQ people have gained some rights in the USA, in Africa, several countries mandate the death sentence for those found to be gay. At home, women still make about 20 percent less per hour than what men make.

> *Any country can create laws,* but until you change the hearts of the people, *the laws don't—and can't— protect as intended.*

It's beyond clear that the USA still needs those deeply committed to equal rights for all. Any country can create laws, *but until you change the hearts of the people*, the laws don't—and can't—protect as intended.

We can do better. What you teach your children matters. The example you set matters. The more you create a love-based home that embraces your responsibility as a global citizen, the more your children will naturally follow your example.

The more all of us respect the sanctity of human life around the globe, the greater our planet will be for all its citizens.

Try This:

1. Make sure you have a globe at home or a world map. When something on the news comes on that involves another country, have your children identify the country on the map. Ask them to look up information on that country on their phones. Make it a game. Who can tell me the population of that country or city? Who can tell me what kind of government they have? Who is the leader of the country? How do they hold elections? What is their relationship with our own country? Get creative. We now have information quite literally at our fingertips. Consciously develop your children's knowledge and curiosity about the larger world. Journal about your experience.

2. Find a cause you can support outside of your own country. Better yet, ask the children in your life to find a cause to support outside of their own country. Find a way to make that happen. We've introduced people to Heifer International. They have a gift book around the holidays where you can give gifts of chickens, ducks, goats and cows to families in other countries. Heifer International does the hard work. You write the check. It's a way to show your kids how much of a difference a chicken or a goat can make in the life of a family in another country, the repercussions of even a small gesture.

3. Begin bringing up global issues and ask, as a family, how can we help? How else might we help? How might our neighborhood help? It might mean changing some habits in your family. This is how you grow critical thinkers.

4. Plan a trip, real or imagined depending on your budget, that exposes your family to another culture. Perhaps it is going to a town that has a large population from another country. Visit ethnic restaurants. Attend international festivals. Learn basic words in that language. Learn some words in the language of the country you are visiting. When Pam speaks with Rwandan people in Kinyarwanda, they are delighted and go as far as her new language skills take her. Most of them speak English as

well, but the effort she makes to converse with them in their native language creates an instant connection.

Double Bonus Try This:

Have a country of the month club in your home. Assign different family members to research foods, clothing, celebrations and more. Together learn basic words from the country being studied. Use those words in your conversations during that month. Culminate each month with a traditional dinner served in your home. Have family members share at least one surprise fact during a family meal each week.

If you have the ability, consider hosting an international student for a semester or sending your own child to a host family in another country when they are in high school. This experience is life changing.

Start (or Join) A Movement

When your heart pulls you forward, you
are fueled by love. Take action.

—*Marci Moore*

Dear You,

You are a whole unto yourself. You are also part of a
greater whole. If you are tempted to think that in the
context of so many you do not measure or matter, I
want you to reconsider. Think about the archer who
misses the target by half an inch; of the politician
who loses by a single vote. A little increment means
the world when the objective is to strike the target.
And one vote can turn an election.

You matter. There is unique talent, skill and ability;
there is an inimitable footprint on the planet; there
is a rare gene combination that walks around with
your name on it. Make more of your marks. Now.
Today. Tomorrow. And then, the tomorrow after that.
Your marks matter.

Love,

Your Life

It's never too late to start or join a movement. Mine is increasing the expression of love on the planet— one person to another. Some people work tirelessly to eradicate bullying one welcoming gesture at a time; others support those experiencing divorce, illness or loss. Some people work to increase access to water in third world countries. Still others build capacity through microloans or business building.

Some people build homes around the globe through Habitat for Humanity International. With the help of social media, both organized and independent movements spread rapidly across borders.

When Mary Anne Radmacher's brother was diagnosed with brain cancer, she asked friends to mail supportive cards and notes to him. Throughout his illness they responded with a mountain of cards and gifts. The daily mail buoyed his spirits. By the time Don passed away, he'd amassed three scrapbooks stuffed with cards he'd received from people the world over. Mary Anne later helped launch The Radmacher Project, a group dedicated to sending cards and notes to individuals facing challenging life situations. Today, Radmacher Project volunteers routinely shower recipients with encouragement and support. A similar group provides emotional support to those facing breast cancer.

Grace Moyd took a trip to Africa. While there she met a large family who broke a single wooden pencil into five pieces because schools mandated children bring their own school supplies. On the trip home, Grace decided no child should miss school for want of a pencil. She came up with a business plan for a card line that allowed her to tell this story and invite others to help fund basic school supplies for school children in Africa. Her company, WritefullyHis, provides supplies to schools in at least four different African countries.

Author and activist Patti Digh, deeply affected by the deaths of several black church members in a racially motivated hate crime, immediately built and offered Hard Conversations, a four week anti-racism teleclass to anyone interested. Rather than sitting at home sobbing, Patti took action. Instead of the couple hundred people she expected to show up, registrations climbed into the thousands.

James Chippendale and Mike Peters started the Love, Hope, Strength Foundation, a leading rock music charity that promotes cancer and leukemia awareness, helps build cancer centers around the world and partners with Delete Blood Cancer to deepen the worldwide donor registry for leukemia patients.

It's your turn. When your heart pulls you forward, you are fueled by love. Pay attention. You don't have to be an entrepreneur. You don't have to have all the answers. That which excites you, ignites you. Start or join a movement.

Laser focus your love. Once you see where there is need, connect. Act.

Try This:

1. Think about the last time you connected with something that mattered in the larger world. How did you take part? Journal about your experience.

2. Plug into where you are passionate. Love animals? Volunteer at your local animal shelter. Act as a foster pet parent or offer to host and train young pups to become service animals. Love people? Plug into any social services agency. Love literacy? Help people learn to read or plug in at your local library. Interested in food insecurity? Volunteer in a food kitchen or connect with Feeding America.

3. Plug in afar. Check into Volunteer Vacations, sign up with Habitat for Humanity International or get up close and personal with Heifer International. Join a mission trip. Support the humanitarian work of others and expand your knowledge of the world at the same time.

4. Start your own movement. What moves you? What gets your juices flowing? What need tugs at your heart but remains under-addressed? Make it happen.

Go Forth

Here is what I know for sure:

> When there is love in our hearts,
> there is love in our homes.
> When there is love in our homes,
> there is love in our communities.
> When there is love in our communities,
> there is hope for the larger world.
> Start a chain reaction of love today.

—Marci Moore

The planet needs you—and all living inhabitants of the planet need you—your love and your zest for life.

Propel yourself into action. You are a loving, compassionate human being. Now go forth. Love with abandon. Live and love with purpose. Start by treasuring yourself enough to strengthen your foundation and keep it strong with purposeful pauses, check-ins and ongoing self-care. Love on those you share your life with in the smallest of daily actions as well as the larger ones, too. Infuse each day with gratitude. Lavishly splash it around. As long as you show up with love for yourself, you'll never run out.

Love on one another in every space in your life: in your home, at work, out in the community, during your commute or picking up the grandkids from soccer practice, in line at the post office and on your travels, near and far.

Build in pockets of time where you can spontaneously offer assistance to others. Those pockets of time are where the magic happens; if you're too busy running from one appointment to the next with no cushion built in between, you'll miss them and you'll miss out.

Love on the larger world with your generous heart. Discover your passionate causes and give something—then give even more of your time, talents or treasures. When you give enough to feel that initial twinge of discomfort yet keep on giving, you'll experience a seismic love shift. Your ability to stretch beyond your comfort zone impacts every area of your life and the lives of others. Your gifts matter to the recipients. Your gifts change lives. Ultimately, your gifts change the world.

The truth is no other person on earth can love exactly like you. No other person offers the same miraculous combination of brilliance, creativity, beauty and heart. You are the only you there is and if we're to make an even bigger difference in this world through love, then we absolutely need your participation.

There is no one who can accomplish what you are here to do. The way that you show up with love is unique in all the world. Start small. Start large. Just start somewhere and start now! Let love carry you onward!

Love onward,
Marci Moore and Mary Anne Radmacher

Acknowledgments

We'd like to thank all those who gave their support (and patience!) while writing this book. First, a big thank you for those who contributed their thoughts to this book: Caren Albers, Ralph Bramucci, Patti Digh, Kathleen Gallagher Everett, Laurie Foley and Lisa Vetter.

You inspire us to continually show up with love.

Those whose fine words start each section, enrich our lives by their deep and practical words. What would any author be without enthusiastic readers? We thank you for reading this book.

Sweetie Berry has danced in at the most necessary times and applied her expertise generously and graciously. Thanks to Paula Lowe for her expert public relations guidance and her support and friendship. Everyone should have a friend as organized and thoughtful as Paula. Barbara Grassey, known as The Book Boss, certainly IS! She brought beautiful order to this book along with the masterful assistance of Euan M., with keen and quick formatting work. Dr. Davis, you know how to make something already sparkly shine ever more brightly. Nicole Pransky, the cover you created reflects Marci's favorite color and the impact of a real letter. The superfans of Marci and Mary Anne's work shared this work broadly and enthusiastically: You KNOW who you are and we are grateful for you shouting from the rooftops! Thanks to all the other angels who stepped in to bring this book to life when life threw Marci a giant curve ball and periodically let me trip.
                                        — *Mary Anne em Radmacher*

With thanks to my family: my wife, Pam, my parents, both writers, for their encouragement and unfailing belief in me, Joel and

Marvin for always making me laugh, Paul for offering bear hugs, Wesley, Joshua, Katie, Clayton, Zachary, Chad and Mikey for being the greatest playdates, movie dates, niece and nephews any aunt could ask for.

Thanks to Tracy Turner for moral support, for being my very first reader and offering up rich, relevant feedback.

Thanks to Dr. Deanna Davis for believing in my message and supporting it in countless ways.

Many thanks to dear friend and co-author Mary Anne Em Radmacher for recognizing and acknowledging something you noticed in my writing all those years ago during my first writing class with you. Thank you for helping me unearth and nurture the writer within. My time at the little red writer's cottage on Whidbey Island where my words flowed onto the page faster than the eagles soaring overhead provided the perfect setting to focus on *Love Letters from Your Life*.

Photo Credit: Cast and Forge Photography

Work With Us

Additional copies of this book can be ordered through most platforms where books are sold.

Marci Moore

Marci Moore is a writer, speaker, an ICF certified coach, love advocate, breast cancer survivor, cyclist, wife, proud aunt of six nephews and one niece, daughter, sister, friend and a member of a very rare species—a Florida native. She is an avid reader, art enthusiast, puzzle queen, world traveler and Life Is A Verb Camp Alumni and devotee. Marci champions people and volunteers as she is able. She most enjoys carrying on conversations with complete strangers and Showing Up with Love, both in her community and wherever she and her wife Pam travel.

Though a huge fan of minimalism and organization, her own house runs on the messy side. She is more apt to spend spare moments on love, fun and time with people, than on organizing.

When she is not writing with a cup of coffee nearby, Marci can be found navigating short sections of the Pinellas County Trail with Pam on their tandem recumbent bike, reading, hanging out with family, connecting with people or taking pictures.

Find Marci: ShowUpWithLove.com

Mary Anne Em Radmacher.

As an artist, Mary Anne has designed hundreds of products in the last three decades and her words and art appear in homes, offices and schools around the globe. As an aphorist and poet, she is quoted in print, media and on social platforms. Her words are used to mark significant life events. She is included in the *Oxford Dictionary of American Quotations*.

Mary Anne is the author of over a dozen books. She consults with clients around the world and delivers trainings in retreat and corporate settings. She is walked regularly by her two dogs and responds well to their commands.

Find Mary Anne: Maryanneradmacher.net

You can find Inspired goods from both Marci and Mary Anne at AppliedInsight.net

CPSIA information can be obtained
at www.ICGtesting.com
Printed in the USA
LVHW090118240919
631983LV00008B/1052/P

9 781733 147101